MEN DON'T JUST EXIST, THEY EXAGGERATE

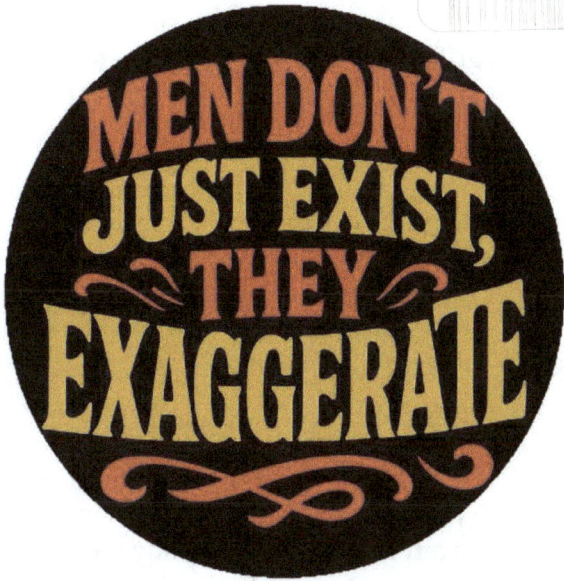

1000+ Ways to Explain Your Manliness

By: A.R. Weston

"This book contains gratuitous amounts of masculinity. Every time a page is turned, a ribeye steak grills itself, and a Bald Eagle sheds a tear of respect."

- A.R. Weston

Men Don't Just Exist, They Exaggerate: 1000+ Ways to Explain Your Manliness
Copyright © 2025 A.R. Weston
www.arweston.com

ISBN: 978-1-949439-17-5

DISCLAIMER

This is a joke book and for entertainment purposes only. The pages you are about to read are satire, humor, nonsensical one-liners, and parody. A few real facts appear in the introduction, based on publicly available information. Nothing in this book is intended to be taken seriously, literally, factually, or as medical advice. If you find yourself searching for actual truths about men, you've come to the wrong place. Get a life, relax, and laugh a little bit.

The artwork in this book was generated through AI using original prompts and creative direction from the author. Any resemblance to real persons, living or dead, or actual events, is purely coincidental.

TABLE OF CONTENTS

Introduction

Let's start with the obvious, this book is entirely ridiculous and outrageous. Everything in this book is made up and in no way is factual, not a single word of it. Well, except maybe a few things that are probably true about you and me. Yes, I have wrestled a crocodile in the Nile River, and yes, it did apologize to me for interrupting my swim. No tomfoolery, my golf swing is so smooth that birds stop midair to admire it.

No, unfortunately, or fortunately in some respects, this book is not filled with any credible or realistic information. Originally, the concept of this book was "1000+ *Interesting Facts About Men*" and the goal was to make every single one of them true. When making the list, I quickly realized I could only find eight that were remotely interesting about men.

- ♂ Heart disease is the leading cause of death in men.
- ♂ Men are more likely to be colorblind.
- ♂ Men's skin produces more oil which increases acne.
- ♂ The sweat glands on a man are more active.
- ♂ Male pattern baldness impacts about 50% of men.
- ♂ A man's resting body temperature is about 98.6 degrees.
- ♂ Men's bodies store fat often around the stomach.
- ♂ A man can reproduce from puberty until death.

Do you see the problem? None of that screams testosterone, grit, and manliness. There is nothing inherently fun about real facts when it comes to explaining raw masculinity. If the claim about a man is not soaked in gratuitous amounts of hyperbole, then what is the point? The real bravado of men is not captured by what is true about a man, but if the thing being said about the man illuminates the point of what is being said.

When was the last time you heard a man tell you all the ways they were average? As men, how we tend to rationalize our ability, skills, and life in general, is best served with a healthy dose of exaggeration. Men adding obscure comparisons, unrealistic scenarios, and crazy outcomes to their stories is not a bad thing. We are not delusional; we are merely embracing the long manly tradition of exaggeration.

Men Exaggerate

The simple truth is that explaining the spirit of manliness lives in exaggeration. Men tend to inflate stories like a cheap blowup doll at a bachelor party. Guys are prone to take the minor and normal challenges of life and turn them into heroic war stories. We never mow the lawn, we tame the earth into submission. We don't tell stories about our fishing line breaking when we hook a slightly bigger than average fish, we create myths for all humanity to admire regarding the ONE that got away. We don't drive to work in the morning; we battle traffic in our steel fortresses on wheels.

There is no such thing as leisurely grilling steaks on the deck because we, as men, are performing a sacred ritual of supplying meat for our family's nourishment. Aliens do visit earth because they worship us due to the enormity of our... personalities. There is no situation that occurs in a man's life that he cannot inflate into something greater.

It is perfectly acceptable for men to exaggerate because it's all in good fun. No one gets hurt due to a little embellishment. Exaggeration isn't only acceptable for men, but it is also essential in how we approach life. We brag, we bond, and we playfully put each other down to boost our own manliness. It's what men do.

Exaggeration vs. Lying

Lying is deceptive, misleading, and immoral. If you find yourself around a man who is a true liar, then get away from that guy. This book in no way is promoting men to lie at the expense of others. Dishonest men are dirtbags and most guys despise them. Exaggeration, on the other hand, should only be used as aspirational and fun. Life is more fun when men embrace exaggeration into their speech with humility and honor as the foundation.

Exaggeration is not lying; it is an art form, like Jazz or belly dancing. Art is not about deception, but about creativity and passion. A man's mundane thought can evolve into a magnificent miracle of human expression. Exaggeration lightens the mood, makes people think, and most importantly, it helps younger men aspire to maximize their potential as a man.

Testosterone-Soaked Non-Sense

You didn't pick up this book because you wanted real facts, right? I sure hope not. You browsed, searched, and scoured around for man-facts, outrageous, embellished, and ridiculously exaggerated ways to describe how you articulate your masculinity. Is anything in this book remotely accurate to depict reality? Not even close, my friend.

This book is your guide to explaining your manly bursting bravado to others. Don't pursue average but instead transcend into a manly myth making legend. Live in a world where men make outrageous claims that future generations will build monuments exemplifying their manly glory.

Now without further ado or delay, flex your twenty-two-inch pythons, grab your sixteen-pound bowling balls, and follow me to the *fountain of masculinity*. Boldly, proudly, hilariously, and dripping with testosterone, here are 1000+ Ways to Explain Your Manliness, because...

Men Don't Just Exist, They Exaggerate!

THE WARM UP:
FART LIKE
A MAN, MY SON!

A well-placed fart is more than a blast of smelly hot air... it is poetry, it is a sonnet, it is a twinkle of hope in a fallen world. Men recount their best farts with a sense of pride while their friends weep in the corner attempting to plug their noses. In olden days, a man would sit in the tavern, lean to the side, and then rattle the windowpanes. With nothing more than a belly full of beer and meat, his farts were declared legendary by the king. His enemies would surrender at the sound of his butt-trumpet.

As the old cliché reminds us, "the man doesn't make the fart, the fart makes the man." Make your ancestors proud! If anyone ever doubts your ability to crack a rat and accuses you of only squeaking them out, don't respond with a non-sulfuric timid answer. Always remember, **men don't just exist, they exaggerate!** Here is a toxic cloud full of ways to respond instead...

♂ My farts scare the crap out of other people.

♂ My farts come with a parental advisory warning.

♂ I once farted and my neighbor's carbon monoxide and fire alarm went off. There were no survivors.

♂ Home renovation companies pay me to peel the paint off the walls, with my farts.

7

♂ I can play the trumpet with my butt cheeks and hit notes only heard from a tuba.

World Record Toot

The world record for longest fart in history lasted almost 3 minutes. Now that is prestigious and worth bragging about! Can you get to 4 minutes?

♂ A fart I let go of in 1992 is still echoing across Europe.

♂ My farts fog up the mirrors in the neighbor's house.

♂ I walked through the woods, and a skunk filed a restraining order.

♂ I farted into my dog's kennel, and he called animal control.

♂ A single fart from me can clear a room, a building, a block, and a full-grown man's brain.

Roland the Farter

Did you know that farting is a respected art form? Henry II, King of England, frequently hired an entertainer named Roland to perform a dance that ended with a loud fart. That's right! You can absolutely make the bold assertion that your farts deserve royal admiration.

♂ My farts are known to boost Wi-Fi signals and disrupt Bluetooth connections.

♂ I can fart the entire alphabet... in Latin.

♂ My farts create more gust and downforce than a jumbo jet during takeoff.

♂ I once farted a sunburn onto my inner thighs.

♂ My farts are called "whispers in the wind" and they smell like regret.

♂ I farted in my sleep and knocked my dog off the bed.

Fart-Flex Formula

$$V = P * ES$$

Volume of Fart = Pressure * Exit Speed

♂ I once farted and gave the toilet seat a hickey.

♂ Moses parted the Red Sea, and I fart-parted the Brown Sea.

♂ NASA once confused my farts with solar flares.

♂ I cracked a windshield with a fart on a car parked on a different street.

♂ I can fart in surround sound that rivals movie theaters.

Thou Old Fart-eth

Did you know that the word "fart" is one of the oldest words in the English language? The original Old English word was "feortan." Your farts transcend history.

♂ When I fart, my smart watch tracks that I am sky diving.

♂ My farts are known to change geese migration patterns.

♂ I can split an atom with my fart like a nuclear bomb, I call them Thermo-Nuka-Toots.

♂ When I burp, a new star is born. When I fart, an old star becomes a black hole.

♂ The local sheriff's office pays me to perform eviction notices with my farts.

♂ I farted in an outhouse and the flies all instantly died.

♂ My farts make dogs seek shelter. They think there is a thunderstorm.

Don't be Average!

Mere mortals are known to fart 14-20 times per day and 99% of their air biscuits are odorless. Unacceptable! If you want to exaggerate properly, you must always claim that you fart over 30 times a day and that only 1% of your duck-rips are not potent.

♂ The EPA makes me register the methane outputs coming from my butt.

♂ Military scientists are currently studying my farts as a potential chemical weapon after chili night.

♂ God forbid I ever fart into a time machine because the past would turn green.

♂ Aliens stopped visiting earth after they abducted and probed me. Good luck to them getting the smell out of their ship.

Fart Fact!

The average person can run about 6 MPH, while a fart leaves your body at 7 MPH. Be sure to remind your runner friends that your farts are faster than them!

♂ I once farted a man out of amnesia and simultaneously made him wish he could forget again.

♂ I liken my farts to love. They are overwhelming, invisible, and they will make you cry.

♂ One of my farts can melt a snowman located in the arctic during winter with a negative windchill.

♂ I have been told by friends that my fart changed their lives, not in a good way, they just wanted me to know.

♂ I have exorcised a haunted house with a single fart. The priest told me that the ghost was gone, but a demon was now present.

Float Some Gas

In case you didn't know, a single fart consists of about 1 cup of gas in volume consisting of hydrogen and methane. Both gases are lighter than air and float upwards. You can 100% declare your farts ascend!

♂ Insurance companies will cancel your homeowner's policy if I fart in your house.

♂ I like to fart into my hand and blow them to my wife. I call them peanut butter kisses!

♂ I farted during a road trip and satellite mapping services removed the town from their database.

♂ The last time I farted in the airport, air traffic control had to reroute all flights because of the cloud.

♂ The pastor banned me from attending the church's annual chili-cook off declaring, "The apocalypse wouldn't even be that bad compared to my farts."

Man vs. Termite

When it comes to quantity, there is simply no competing with the mighty flatulence of the termite. Termites produce around 11% of all methane gas in our environment due to their farting. Who knew that wood was the magical fruit?

I once farted a power outage!

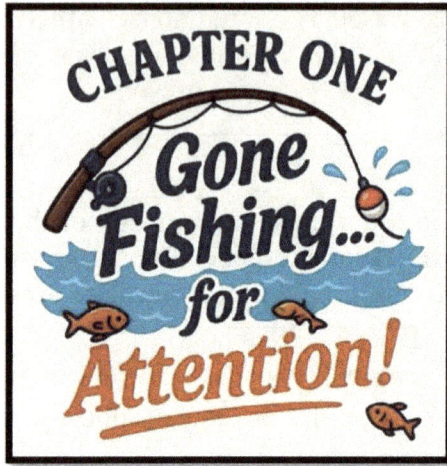

CHAPTER ONE

Gone Fishing... for Attention!

There is a funny feeling that every man gets in their stomach when his sentence begins with, "You should have seen the fish I caught...". All men transform from a modest fisherman into an extreme angler when they initiate a fishing story. Sure, we didn't get a picture but take our word for it. The fish was out of this world impressive. And if we say it was a 10-pound bluegill, then it was probably more like 15 pounds because we are modest.

A good fishing story demands embellishment, and men are well equipped to rise to the position of majestic mythmaker. There is always that one guy or gal that calls us a liar. Shame on them for doubting our angling proficiencies. If someone ever calls into doubt your ability to drown a worm, then don't settle for an insignificant response. Always remember, **men don't just exist, they exaggerate!** Here is a tackle box full of ways to respond instead...

♂ I don't have to use bait or lures, fish jump into my boat when they hear my name.

♂ My fishing line is stronger than titanium and smoother than silk. It's made from my chest hair.

♂ I have caught sharks by fiercely gazing into the ocean and yelling "come".

12

♂ I can fillet and grill a fish while it is still on the line.

♂ Fish ask me for an autograph before I release them back into the lake.

A Reel Spinner

When it comes to speed, there is no comparison to the fastest anglers on record who reel in more than 15 fish in a minute. Exaggerate your cast and blast capabilities by saying you could catch 20 fish in a minute, if you tried.

♂ The ocean sends me thank you cards for eating all the weak fish.

♂ One of my recent catches whispered to me that fish check the weather and cancel their weekend plans when they know I am on the lake.

♂ Prize fish have a lottery to see who has the privilege of being caught by me.

♂ The last fish I netted was so big it had its own zip code.

♂ Poseidon prostrates himself on the ocean floor when I am fishing. He respects and worships me!

Fishy Bragging Rights

One of the biggest fish ever caught was a White Sturgeon weighing 1000 pounds and was 12 feet long. Your chance of catching something bigger than that is slim to none. The average freshwater fish is well under 5 pounds. Always remember, if you want to impress your buddies when exaggerating your day at the lake, always go bigger than average!

♂ The fish I catch at the public pool are bigger than the ones you catch in the ocean.

♂ I hooked a largemouth bass, a catfish, and a rainbow trout all with a single cast, and they were in different lakes.

♂ I use a fish finder to track fish, but they use satellite imagery to try and avoid me.

♂ During a fishing trip to Alaska, I taught a bear how to catch a fish.

♂ I could ice fish, without cutting a hole in the ice, and still catch bigger fish than you.

Endurance Angling

Do you have stamina and intestinal fortitude? If so, then you may qualify to call yourself an endurance angler. While not an official sport, it is still a respectful title. To earn this title, you must be able to fish at minimum 14 hours at a time without breaks. Of course, you could always exaggerate!

♂ Scientists were shocked at the last fish I caught because they thought it was an eighth continent I pulled from the bottom of the ocean.

♂ Fish fillet, fry, and cover themselves in tartar sauce out of respect for me.

♂ Extinct species have resurrected back into existence to have an opportunity for me to catch them.

♂ I am banned from entering all aquariums because the fish have a heart attack when I enter the building.

♂ I catch fish so big that they have satellites orbiting them.

Maximum Depth

Crater Lake in Oregon is the deepest lake in the USA at a little less than 2000 feet deep. Most lakes are nowhere near that depth. If you want to impress, exaggerate the time it took for the bait to hit the bottom. Say "it took 45 seconds for your bait to hit the bottom with a 2-ounce sinker." That will get their attention!

♂ I trained a fish to walk so I could catch him again on dry land.

♂ The last fish I caught was so big it dragged me through time.

♂ I hunted the fish that ate Jonah and brought the tartar sauce with me.

Angler Math (Bro-Quantum Theory)

$$FS = AC * ST^2 / R$$

$$\text{Fish Size} = \frac{\text{Alcohol Consumed} * (\text{Story Telling})^2}{\text{Reality}}$$

♂ I caught a fish so big that the water level lowered when I pulled it out of the lake.

♂ I caught a fish so big that the Navy accused me of stealing a submarine.

♂ Aliens travel to earth because they heard stories of a famous intergalactic angler.

♂ I caught a fish so big it was measured with a football field.

♂ The ocean sued me for violating maritime law for catching excessive amounts of fish on a single pole.

♂ Fish sing sea-shanties about my life and being caught by me.

How Big is Your Pole?

Fishing poles come in a wide variety of lengths and girths. While longer may indicate better big game performance, real anglers know that girth is equally important. After all, you wouldn't go whaling with a tiny pole. A good size depends on what you hope to catch. Always smile and remember, there is someone with a smaller pole than you!

♂ I am such a fishing legend that people refer to my secret fishing spot as Atlantis and my rod as Poseidon's trident.

♂ I catch so many fish that the ocean sends me an annual cease-and-desist letter.

♂ The fish I catch are so big I must file them as dependents on my tax return.

♂ I am such a respected angler that I pulled a fish from the lake, and it called me "captain" then showed me a tattoo with my name in the middle of its fin.

♂ I caught a fish so big that it threw me into the water and is now dating my wife.

♂ I fought a fish so long the moon changed phases, twice.

♂ When I fish at night, I catch so many fish I can see the man on the moon wet his pants.

Stinky Fingers

Ever wonder why fish stink? That smell after a long day of catching fish is due to a chemical called trimethylamine oxide. When a fish dies, the smell increases rapidly due to bacteria and enzymes. Why do you need to know this? Well, you don't, but now you do and feel free to exaggerate your knowledge of fish biology.

♂ I tried catch and release, but the fish kept begging to come home with me.

♂ The last fish I caught was so big that it had a verified account on social media.

♂ The lakes I fish on put "for sale" signs up after I leave.

♂ The last fish I caught left me with a 5-star review on my dating profile.

♂ I hooked a fish so big that it tilted the Earth off its axis by 3 degrees.

♂ I caught a fish last summer that was so big it had three kids, a wife, and was having a midlife crisis.

♂ My boat trailer has been used to transport the fish I catch. I carry the boat home on my shoulder.

Let's Get Mythical, Mythical!

The best way to exaggerate your catch is with a good analogy. Instead of saying, "It was the size of a whale," take the hyperbole to the next level by using mythical comparisons. "I caught Namazu," a legendary Japanese monster. "I hooked a Makara," a beast, from India, responsible for guarding ancient temples.

Reel Tip: If all else fails, say, "I landed your mom last night" and your friends will understand.

I am the reason the Loch Ness Monster is hiding!

CHAPTER TWO

A BEARD IS A DECLARATION OF MANHOOD!

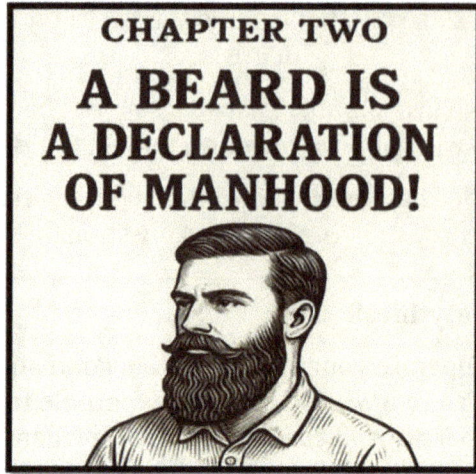

Birds create nests, beavers build dams, and men grow beards. There is a special connection between a man and his beard. Whether it is peach fuzz, stubble, patchy, or glorious, it is the property of the man that wears it. A birthright of all men is the hair that grows on their face. Barbers bow before a magnificent beard. Hairdressers weep and tremble when a superb mane enters their shop.

There is always that one clean shaven guy that mocks and scowls at another man's beard. Shame on him and his family for they know not what they do. Be sure to unfriend him on social media and do not invite him to your birthday party. When anyone makes a comment or asks you about your beard, don't settle for some snowflake reply. Always remember, **men don't just exist, they exaggerate.** Respond like this instead...

♂ My beard is so full that it blocks cell phone tower signals.

♂ If I get lost in the woods, I can survive by taking shelter in my beard.

♂ Birds apply for permits to build their nest in my beard.

♂ The beard of my shadow is nicer than your beard.

♂ The beard under my beard is better than your beard.

Victorian Era

During the Victorian Era, a large bushy beard was a symbol of manliness. Want to look and feel more masculine? Grow a beard!

♂ An angel gets its wings every time I stroke my beard, and every time I shed hair from my beard, a demon is cast into hell.

♂ Barbers follow me when I go out and ask me for a selfie with my beard.

♂ Razors become instantly dull when they see my beard.

♂ I have been banned from the shaving aisle in every major retail store because of my beard.

♂ Santa Claus quit giving out gifts at Christmas when he saw how a man grows a beard.

Copper Whiskers

Did you know that beard hair is ridiculously strong and is comparable to copper wire when it is the same thickness? That's right, bearded warrior. Your face is practically covered in metal, and you should tell everyone about it.

♂ My beard has been registered as a world heritage site, twice.

♂ If you take a picture of my beard and zoom in, then you will see that my beard is growing another beard.

♂ If you pump a wind gust through my beard it comes out the other side as a slight breeze.

♂ I can remove the paint off a truck using only the stubble from my beard.

A.R.'s Beard Proverbs

- ✓ A man without a beard is a lion without a mane, still a man, but without credibility or confidence.
- ✓ Never trust a beardless man, for he shaves away his honor and displays a naked chin.
- ✓ Don't count your chickens before they hatch, unless you have a beard.

♂ My go-to beard oil is 5W30 and I change it every 3000 miles.

♂ The nation of Denmark tried to make my beard their king.

♂ I came out of the womb with a 5 o'clock shadow.

Combat Ready

Ever wonder why the military insists on a clean-shaven face? The tradition of soldiers shaving goes back to Alexander the Great. Enemy combatants could grab a beard and use it as an advantage during combat.

Warrior Wisdom: If you are unable or unwilling to grow a beard, exaggerate that you're not a baby face, but you are simply combat ready!

♂ I have a pet attack squirrel that lives in my beard, his nickname is Big Nuts.

♂ Cops pull me over to compliment my beard, and I write them a ticket for being unworthy.

♂ Yesterday I shaved my face with a chainsaw and used motor oil for shaving cream.

♂ Bald Eagles try to build their nests in my beard because it is so majestic.

♂ Santa asked me for advice on how to make his beard whiter and more dignified.

Razors Waste Time

Do you hate wasting time? Shaving accounts for over 3000 hours of a man's life. That is over 125 days of your life you are throwing away on shaving off your glorious mane. If anyone ever questions you for growing a beard, remind them that they are wasting their life shaving. Be time efficient and grow a beard like a man!

♂ I don't grow my beard; my beard grows me.

♂ I have found a treasure map in my beard. I followed the treasure map and it led me back to my beard.

♂ Razors instantly turn into butter knives when they see my beard.

Socrates & Plato

Greek philosophers considered beards to be a physical representation of their wisdom, brilliance, and dignity. That's right, you handsome bearded stud, ancient history insists on you keeping the beard forever!

Fact-ish: A beard increases IQ points, EQ points, and Credit Score.

♂ The Vikings wrote battle hymns about the glory of my beard.

♂ My beard is so thick and luscious it forms microclimates.

♂ My beard once caught a frisbee on accident.

♂ When my beard brushes my wife's face it exfoliates her soul.

Hair Follicle Productivity (HFP) Model

$$C = BL * G - S$$

Confidence = Beard Length * Genetics - Shaving

♂ Birds chirp louder when they see my beard. They think heaven has come down to earth.

♂ My beard comb is made from a porcupine pelt.

♂ My beard clippings are frequently used to texture truck bed liners.

♂ I never use mirrors because my beard reflects the truth.

♂ My beard's wi-fi password is "Respect-The-Growth."

Pharaoh Approved

Did you know that ancient Egyptians wore fake beards made of metal as a sign of divinity? That's right... Pharaoh would even be jealous of that immaculate beard on your face.

♂ The trees whisper, "He's one of us!" when I walk into the forest.

♂ My beard is so long I get it caught in the escalator, on the floor beneath me.

♂ My beard is so long I once got it tangled in my shoelaces.

♂ My beard is so long I must use a leaf blower to dry it after the shower.

♂ My beard is so long I get it caught in my zipper.

♂ My beard is a battle cry for freedom.

Honest Abe's Beard

Most of his life, Abraham Lincoln remained a baby face. It was not until an 11-year-old punked him that he decided to grow his iconic beard. He lost eight key elections, grew a beard, and became President of the United States.

Presidential Pro-Tip: A patchy beard is better than no beard. The power of the beard is undeniable, only if you want to be successful in life, of course!

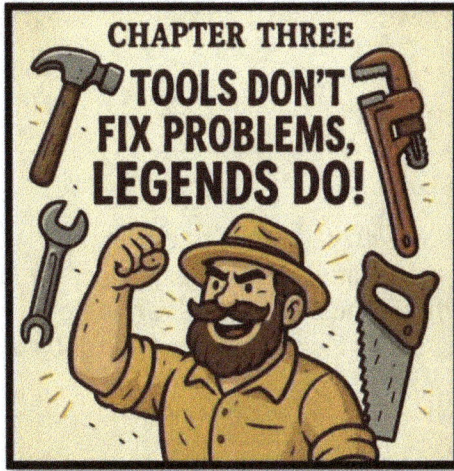

CHAPTER THREE

TOOLS DON'T FIX PROBLEMS, LEGENDS DO!

Men know that when it comes to tools, we don't use them, but we *become* them. All day long at work, what do we think about?... That project in the garage, of course! The joy of wielding our tools like a blue-collar warrior. Picture it, smell the sweet sawdust wafting through the garage with the game on in the background. Every tool is polished, organized, and ready to be used for its specific purpose. You grunt and crack open another cold one. Life in the garage is the only life worth living!

Your buddy, who comes over to watch the game, looks around in amazement. He asks, "Hey bro, do you know how to use all of them tools you got?" Responding with a simple, "yes" would work, but would that do justice to your passion for your ability to fix things or your love of tools? When someone asks you about your ability to use tools or your ability to fix things, don't settle for some flimsy modest answer. Always remember, **men don't just exist, they exaggerate**. Respond like this instead...

♂ My tools stand at attention and salute when I enter the garage.

♂ Broken appliances fix themselves when I walk into the room.

♂ The battery on my drill is charged with testosterone injections and raw masculinity.

23

♂ All my tools were handmade from rocks and the will to survive.

♂ I can change my oil while I am driving.

Sharpen Your Own Blades

A quick, simple, and cost-effective way to exaggerate your manliness is to always sharpen your own blades, axe heads, knives, or lawn mower blades. Learn how to use a whetstone, honing rod, or angle grinder. Not only can you brag to your buds about always having a sharp blade, but you can also save a ton of cash.

♂ I can install a new door so well that it will open to other dimensions.

♂ Last year I rebuilt my truck's engine, blindfolded, and with one arm tied behind my back.

♂ I fix things before they know they are broken.

♂ The only thing I need to fix a car is an Allen key and glue.

♂ I can carve a tree into a new kitchen table without cutting it down.

Collect Them All

There are approximately ten thousand different tools on the market these days. While most men only have a minuscule amount in their garage, don't be an underachiever. A man must have at minimum seventy-five tools in their garage to be considered above average. Tell other guys you have a couple hundred tools and that alone establishes your manliness.

♂ I can drive through a construction site and finish the project without even stopping my truck.

♂ With tape and a socket wrench, I can fix a broken heart.

♂ My loofah is steel wool, and my soap is used motor oil.

♂ No plunger needed because I can clog the toilet and unclog it with the same dump.

♂ Mechanics pay me to loosen bolts, and I never have to use a wrench.

Tool Trivia

Could you name all the tools in your garage? Here is an easy tip to help you exaggerate your knowledge of tools. Learn a little bit of history about a few unique tools, then challenge your pals to a quick game of tool trivia. Ask friends to hold up any tool and then walk them through the historical use of the tool. Your buddies will learn something, and you will look like a tool guru.

♂ Instructions only exist so that I can tear them up and throw them in the trash.

♂ When I enter the hardware store, I can hear the tools whisper "Oh no, he's back."

♂ I could finish a house with nothing but drywall and chewing gum.

♂ I once converted a flat tractor tire into a trampoline for my kids.

♂ I once carved a log into a reclining chair without using a knife.

Measuring Tool Proficiency

$$M = T * (K + H) / E$$

$$\text{Manliness} = \frac{\text{Tools} * (\text{Know} + \text{How})}{\text{Experience}}$$

♂ I once dammed a river using tape and an old pair of boxers.

25

♂ Blacksmiths mistake my family jewels for anvils.

♂ I use a spark plug for a toothpick and a shop rag for a handkerchief.

♂ My toolbox is a 55-gallon steel drum filled with blood, sweat, and tears.

Think Bigger

The biggest hand tools on the market are pipe wrenches. Of the pipe wrench tool family, the biggest and best is the 60 inch. That's five feet of torque power. Even if you never use it, put one on your wall to display the king of hand tools. Show other men yours is bigger than theirs.

♂ The National Landmarks Agency listed my garage on the top 10 list of manliest places in the world.

♂ My tape measure always shows that I have an extra inch more than you.

♂ I once fixed the landing gear on a plane midflight.

♂ I dropped my toolbox in Iowa and it registered an earthquake in Texas.

♂ I have so many tools that my shed has a shed for its tools.

Damn Electricity, You Scary!

Electricity can be scary to work with and when in doubt, always hire a professional. An easy exaggeration tip when it comes to electric is to use vague language in describing your ability. For example, if you say, "I do all my own electric," it could technically mean you change all your own lightbulbs, or it could mean you wired your whole house. It is not your problem how your friend interprets the phrase.

♂ My garage had to be rezoned as commercial real estate because of how many tools I have.

♂ My generator has a backup generator for its generator.

♂ If you need a tool, then I probably have it. If I don't have it, then I have the tools to make it.

♂ I own a toothbrush that has adjustable torque settings.

♂ I once threw my garage a baby shower when I bought a new set of power tools.

Get Hammered!

The first "real" tool ever discovered by historians was the hammer. What a great way to appreciate the vital manly instinct of using tools. Since the start of time, men have desired to hit and smash things. When bragging about your tools, don't forget to drop this fact. Make your ancestors proud!

♂ When I walk past something broken, my pliers start humming and my hammer dances on my tool belt.

♂ I keep a backup set of tools under my pillow at night for safety.

♂ I don't believe in garage sales because selling something out of my garage is against my religion.

♂ I don't change the oil, I give the car life because I am a gracious tool lord.

♂ My toolbelt is the godfather of my neighbor's grandson.

♂ It is written in my will that my tools are buried with me and that I am laid to rest using a forklift.

Togas and Toolbelts

Roman soldiers didn't only carry swords on their belts. The concept of carrying utility tools across your waist has been a tradition since the time of Caesar. Romans would use their belts (cingulum) to holster a variety of tools. That is why the expression is, "When in Rome… wear a toolbelt!"

CHAPTER FOUR
MY GRILL IS BETTER THAN YOURS!

Grilling is a primal art form that perfectly blends fire, smoke, and masculinity. The grill is not about cooking, it is commanding the flames to your will. The steak does not see you as a mortal, but as a deity. It's been a long week. The charcoal is hot and producing the right amount of smoke you desire. Lesser men are boiling a chicken right now, but not you. You are igniting glory!

When your neighbor pops his head over the fence and says, "Oh, that smells delightful. Are you any good at grilling?" A cold nerve runs down your shoulder, into your leg, and you get a slight cramp in your foot. The audacity of that guy to have the stones to ask **YOU** such a question. When someone asks you about your ability to grill, don't settle for some feeble response. Always remember, **men don't just exist, they exaggerate**. Respond like this instead...

♂ When I grill a steak, the cow comes back to life and thanks me for giving it purpose.

♂ I can cook a steak so perfectly that it will make a vegan question everything.

♂ The smoke from my grill spells out my name to show reverence.

♂ I can turn a frozen dinner into a 5-star meal with my grill.

♂ I only eat cereal that has spent 4 hours on the smoker.

Big Flames, Big Claims

We all agree that gigantic flames bursting up from a grill gets blood flowing. Did you know that flame size matters? A steady blue flame that is about an inch high is perfect for grilling. Flames that get too big are a result of excessive grease drip and this may over-char the meat.

♂ I can marinate a steak simply by whispering to it.

♂ I start my grill with lightning and cook with gasoline.

♂ The grill marks on my seared steak can be seen from outer space.

♂ I never flip my burgers, they flip on their own out of respect.

♂ I add two teaspoons of lighter fluid to my chili recipe to help bring down the heat.

The Perfect Touch

A man needing a thermometer might as well hold up a banner that says, "I am a rookie at grilling." The real grill expert only needs one tool to tell if his steak is cooked perfectly, his finger! Knowing when a steak is cooked perfectly is all about how it feels. Practice by touching your index finger to your thumb, that's the same "feel" a medium rare steak should have. If the steak is too springy, it's rare; if it's firm, then it's closer to well done.

♂ I can catch a bullet using broken kitchen tongs.

♂ The only way I deep fry anything is in lava.

♂ I grilled a hot dog last night and got a movie deal.

♂ Last Thanksgiving I cooked the turkey on a hibachi grill, on a kayak, in the middle of a hurricane.

♂ I can tenderize steak by clapping my hands and stomping my feet.

Homer's Wiener

In the 8th century, Homer wrote "The Odyssey" and may have invented the concept of the hotdog. There is a line in Book 20 that describes a sausage being cooked over a fire. Although we do not know the exact size of Homer's wiener, we can assume that it was slathered in ketchup.

♂ Bigfoot is hiding because he knows that my plan is to BBQ him one day.

♂ My potatoes are boiled in acid rain.

♂ My favorite spatula in the kitchen is a crowbar.

♂ The only type of charcoal I use is ancient, petrified wood from forbidden forests.

King of the Grill

Grilling glory does not always come cheap. A good price range for a grill is between $400.00 - $800.00. This isn't a book about saving money; this is a book about exaggerating! A high-end grill costs upwards of $2500. When your buddies ask how much your grill costs you, say a "couple grand" to impress them.

♂ I trained to be a grill guru under Hephaestus, the Greek god of fire.

♂ My meat is seasoned using only the purest salt shipped overnight from the Himalayas.

♂ I can tell how well a steak is cooked by how the smoke tingles my nostrils.

♂ I don't use a timer, but instead I listen to the sweet whisper of the meat.

♂ I marinate my meat by playing Beethoven's 5th to it. The harmony is a natural tenderizer.

The Cavemen Beat Their Meat

The quest for tender meat has been around since the stone age. Cavemen would use large rocks to beat their meat, breaking down the tissue, thus making the meat more tender. Don't feel ashamed if you beat your meat before going out to the grill. Enjoying tenderized steak is a manly tradition.

♂ Every July 4th, I cook a 92-ounce steak and brand it with the outline of a Bald Eagle.

♂ NASA has sent me letters complaining that the smoke ring from my grill blocks their view of earth.

♂ The first and only time my father ever cried was from eating brisket from my smoker because of its tenderness.

♂ I can tell when a steak is perfectly cooked by listening to the frequency of its sizzle.

♂ My grilling apron is stitched together from the aprons of lesser grillers that I have defeated.

Rub Your Meat!

Researchers have found evidence that men have been using fire pits to cook meat for thousands of years. Likewise, the use of rubs and seasoning has always been an important step. An easy bragging tip is to make your own meat rub spice blend. When other guys tell you their favorite brand of seasoning bought at the store, remind them that you only rub your meat with the best.

♂ My grill was forged from the turret of an old Navy battleship.

♂ I cook like my ancestors did; I never follow a recipe but follow instinct only.

♂ While my son was being born, I was outside of the hospital grilling him his first ribeye steak.

♂ For tongs I use channel locks, and my go-to steak knife is a sharpened samurai sword.

♂ My spatula has a higher body count than a Green Beret.

Spartan Warrior

When it comes to manliness, there is no substitute for the Spartans. Fortunately, the spear throwing, sword wielding, shield bearing warriors of old loved to grill. Archeologists have found evidence that ancient Greeks used iron and bronze spits to roast cuts of meat.

♂ I can cook a brisket so well that it calls me daddy.

♂ The flame on my grill kisses the meat I cook like it owes it money.

♂ The rub I give my meat is so good, it will make a vegetarian moan.

BBQ Sauce is Based, Literally!

Base Type	Primary Origins	Best With
Tomato-Based	Kansas City, Memphis, Midwest	Ribs, Chicken, Brisket
Vinegar-Based	Eastern North Carolina, Coastal Carolina	Pulled or Chopped Pork,
Mustard-Based	Central South Carolina	Pork Shoulder, Ribs
Mayonnaise or Butter-Based	Northern Alabama (Tennessee Valley)	Chicken, Turkey

The onions starts to cry when I chop them.

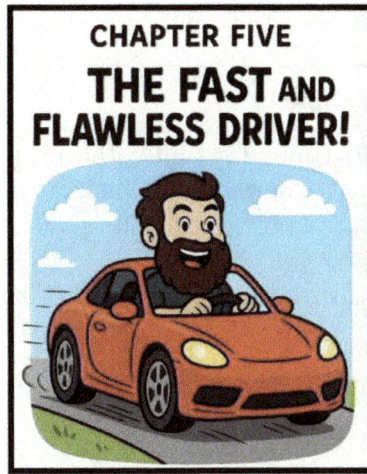

CHAPTER FIVE

THE FAST AND FLAWLESS DRIVER!

A man doesn't drive a car, he operates with precision. The engine, transmission, axles, and low-profile tires always guarantee a smile. A speed limit is nothing more than a suggestion and there is no ticket big enough that will divert him from being an animal on the road. Getting behind the wheel is not about getting from Point A to Point B, no sir. Driving is about freedom and owning the road. Manliness is not found in the passenger seat!

Speed, power, and torque... is there anything else in life worth talking about? Burning out, redlining, and downshifting are the prerequisites for joy. When someone asks you about your driving abilities never settle for some limp idle answer. Always remember, **men don't just exist, they exaggerate**. Respond like this instead...

♂ When I drive on the interstate, traffic parts like the Red Sea, the heavens open, and angels sing.

♂ I never follow road signs, but they follow me and beg for lessons on how to drive.

♂ I once hit the gas so hard my shadow begged me to slow down.

♂ I am the first man to take the driver's test in reverse, blindfolded, and on ice. Passed with a perfect score.

♂ The turn signals in my truck blink to the beat of my heart.

RPM: Raw Power Machine

Did you know that a Formula 1 car hits 60 MPH in 2 seconds, revs to 15,000 RPM, pulls 6 G's in the corners, and stops from 200 MPH in under 5 seconds? You needed to know, that's all!

♂ I could drift a dump truck filled with eggs and not even one will crack.

♂ My driving is so smooth that when I drive through a thunderstorm, mother nature calms down.

♂ I never check for blind spots, they check me.

♂ I top my gas tank off with confidence.

♂ I once parallel parked into a spot so tight, I accidentally split an atom.

'Ello Governor

Most normal vehicles on the road have an electronic governor that restricts high speeds. Even if the speedometer says 160 mph, the darn thing will likely never go that fast. How depressing, right? While removing an electronic governor is not always realistic, at least you can steer clear of exaggerating yourself into an easy to disprove corner.

Tuner Tip: Play it safe, exaggerate top speeds with caution when you are trying to impress your pals, or they will call bull!

♂ Auto manufacturers have requested to study my brain for their self-drive systems.

♂ My tires never lose traction because they are afraid to squeal.

♂ Beethoven's 5th was inspired by the sound of me shifting gears.

♂ I can park my truck between two cars that are driving at highway speeds.

♂ Raceways banned me last year for performance enhanced driving.

Muffled Dreams

The history of men admiring loud cars started in the 1920's. Fast forward 100 years and guys still love the aggressive rumble of an aftermarket exhaust. Stock exhaust is like hitting the mute button on horsepower.

What do you call a man with stock exhaust? Snooze Tubes, Library Exhaust, and Tailpipe Whisperer

---

♂ I once drove so fast that the radio started buffering.

♂ Hollywood has produced action movie scenes based on me driving to the grocery store.

♂ Potholes instantly turn into wishing wells when my tires get too close.

♂ My driving is so smooth that I fill a cup with water and coffee beans and it brews itself.

♂ When I pass a cop doing 100, they pull themselves over for being inadequate.

Preheat the Oven

Only novice gearheads start their car or truck on a cold day and launch out of the parking lot like a bat out of hell. Cold oil doesn't lubricate well and the engine's computer system limits power output when not at optimal temperature. Driving hard on a cold motor puts a lot of stress on your vehicle.

Alpha-Male Advice: Car guys know the importance of preheating their performance machine's oven. The main point is don't be auto-illiterate.

♂ I once turned a roundabout into a square with my perfect cornering.

♂ Toll booths pay me to drive on their roads.

♂ I can parallel park a monster truck between two shopping carts, blindfolded.

♂ I have never used GPS because I tell the road where I want to go.

♂ Never in my life have I been lost; the map is simply wrong.

Burn Rubber

Shortly after World War II, the hot rod era kicked off. The art of doing a burnout, or spinning your tires to create smoke, is a result of too much throttle. Drag racers quickly learned that heating up the tires with a quick spin caused them to heat up and lay down rubber on the road. Thus, the car would have more grip when it launched.

Throttled Excuse: A burnout is not only for fun or showing off, but also practical and should be encouraged!

♂ I passed a super car on the interstate going 100 mph, in a golf cart.

♂ I taught my truck to heel like a well-trained German Shepherd.

♂ I once jumpstarted my truck using static electricity from my butt cheeks.

♂ My truck's oil never needs to be replaced; I whisper "sweet nothings" to it, and it keeps working.

♂ My motorcycle is built out of steel and testosterone.

♂ The engine in my truck runs on nitroglycerine.

♂ I once turned a rusted-out wheelbarrow into a race car.

It's Riddle Time

I am taller than a building with a jaw made of steel. My tail shoots smoke and I get a weekly soak. My owner wants to put me in a shed, but the driveway is forever my bed. Everywhere I go, people stop and stare, and I have more testosterone than a full-grown grizzly bear. What am I?

Answer: A Lifted Truck

♂ I backed into a stranger's driveway so well that the owners came out and gave me a standing ovation.

♂ I removed my turn signals from my truck because the universe already knows which way I am going.

♂ My hair gel is engine grease.

♂ I can drive from L.A. to New York without breaks, not even for my own thoughts.

Zero to Hero

Do you want to go fast or do you want to be quick? Thankfully, these days you don't necessarily need to choose. A modern sports car can do 0-60 in less than 3 seconds and has a top speed exceeding 140MPH.

Redline Reminder: Know your car's stats. If you make up something unrealistic about your ride, you will get called out!

♂ I can drive a stick shift without touching the clutch. I operate on pure instinct and dedication to perfection.

♂ I was pulled over for speeding and gave the cop a ticket for disturbing greatness.

♂ I am so fast I won a drag race riding a wheelbarrow.

♂ I use engine oil as a lubricant, for everything!

♂ I can tune an engine by putting my ear on the garage door.

Mona Lisa on Wheels

When you think of classic Italian art, what comes to mind? A guy named Leonardo? Nah! Super cars is the correct answer. The Italians have conquered pasta, opera, and getting to 200 MPH. There is a reason why Italian sports cars reign supreme and it's because cars in Italy are an expression of art, emotion, and lifestyle. The Italians pioneered the use of carbon fiber bodies, hand-built engines, and mid-engine production platforms

Wisdom Pit Stop: Learn the names of Italian sports cars to impress your friends!

♂ My truck's horn only plays rock'n'roll guitar riffs.

♂ When I was a baby and had a cold, the doctor treated me with diesel exhaust breathing treatments.

♂ The recliner in my man cave has bigger tires than your truck.

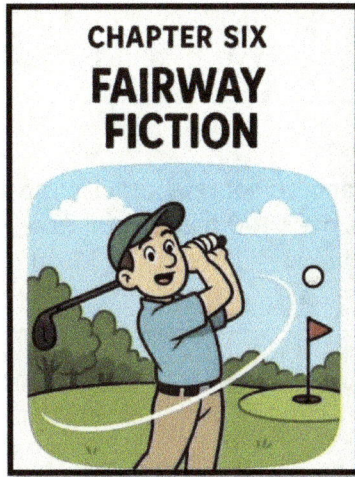

CHAPTER SIX
FAIRWAY FICTION

Golf is a game of precision, power, and prestige. The ancient manly art of embellishment may have been born out on the green. The magic that happens between the first swing to the final putt of the 18th hole is an indescribable feeling. A round of golf filled with duffed shots, slices, lost balls, and questionable scoring, evolves into a story of hole-in-ones, amazing drives, and scores that would make the pros weep with envy.

When someone asks if you are good at golfing, don't tell them the truth that you played in the sandbox at shank city. Let them know how good you are at golfing. Always remember, **men don't just exist, they exaggerate**. Respond like this instead...

♂   I drive a ball so hard that it time-travels and lands before my swing is finished.

♂   My tee-off goes so far, it requires a passport.

♂   I don't slice or hook, I give my ball the creative freedom to go where it wishes.

♂   I can chip, text, and clean my balls all at the same time.

♂ I once hit a hole-in-one from the parking lot before my truck came to a complete stop.

Putting Pro-Ish

The average putting distance is somewhere around 15 to 20 feet. The world record for longest putt is over 400 feet. When exaggerating your putting dominance, it is good to know that less than 5% of golfers can sink a putt from 30 feet.

♂ When I swing, the clubhouse lowers the lights and plays soft music, as if I were making love to the course.

♂ It is normal for even the grass to clap for me when I tee-off.

♂ The only thing more accurate than GPS is my chip shot.

♂ The most advanced AI on the planet asks me for advice on how to play golf like a pro.

Golf-Bellishment

The average male amateur golfer can drive the ball about 230 yards off the tee. If you want to impress, say, "around 305" when asked how far you can hit. It's believable if they don't ask you to prove it!

♂ I don't putt, I snipe the hole with deadly precision.

♂ When you play, the people yell "Fore!" When I play, my fans scream, "Incoming!"

♂ The military is studying my drive to better understand how anti-gravity works.

♂ Mathematicians have drafted dissertations and bet their careers on how straight a line my putt produces.

♂ I don't hit the ball, I seduce the course hole by hole.

♂ I read the curves of the golf course and make the green scream "birdie."

Check Your Balls

Contrary to what most people believe, not all golf balls are created the same. A two-piece ball with a rubber core will travel farther than a tour level ball designed to spin. Knowing this is a great opportunity to dominate driving distance off the tee. Always check your balls before you play with them.

♂ People tell me that my tee-off is better than Christmas morning and more valuable than their first born child.

♂ My short game is not the best, but I always finish quickly, and you bet I always get applause.

♂ My caddie worships the ground that I walk on, literally.

♂ My drive teases my intentions, my chip is a flirt, and my putt seals the deal.

---

27 Hole Course

While it is common knowledge that golf courses have 18 holes, there are some with 27 holes. The concept of the extra 9 holes is that golfers may mix up which holes they want to play. Golfers tend to live by the mantra, "The more holes the merrier."

♂ My 3-wood knows me so well it starts to moan when I unzip the bag.

♂ My long game is tighter than your mom's jeans after a buffet.

♂ I have three security guards for my golf bag and I just hired a fourth.

♂ The clubhouse owner asked me if I would autograph the green on the course's par 5.

♂ People call me the human laser pointer because my putts are so straight.

Epic Hype

Add a little pep to your golfing step and a little swag to your swing. Wear top brands, brag about your short game, and insist that you have been taking classes from a former pro-golfer. Share with your buddies that you are normally a 7 handicap, when you play regularly, of course. Hype it up, baby!

♂ Other golfers think my ball and the hole have magnets on them because my shots always stick perfectly.

♂ My golf swing is too smooth for human ears to hear.

♂ My slices are straighter than most golfer's line drives.

♂ When I go to the driving range, I can hear the golf balls begging to be in my bucket.

Always Loosen Up, With A Drink

Philosophers of old say, "A golfer needs a drink because sobriety is never par for the course." In all seriousness, kicking back a few may sometimes be an advantage for some golfers. Always remember, calming the nerves with a few cold ones is not the same thing as streaking across the back nine after a fifth of bourbon. It's all about moderation!

♂ "Bunkers, sand traps, and roughs," are not words in my vocabulary.

♂ The wind that my swing produces rivals an F5 tornado.

♂ I have hit more birdies than a city bus.

♂ Every course I play on rolls out the red carpet and plays entrance music for me.

♂ I am the first man to hit the horizon with a golf ball.

How Golf Took Flight?

Birdie, Eagle, Albatross, and Condor? What's up with all the bird names in golf? Well, the answer to that is that it all started in the late 1800's when using the word "bird" referred to something exceptional. Golfers kept the bird theme and the names took flight, both literally and figuratively.

♂ Even at dawn my caddie wears sunglasses to keep the brilliance of my golf game from blinding him.

♂ Eagles and Birdies refer to my scorecard as a migration map.

♂ Course owners insist that I play an extra 19th hole alone to keep scores close.

♂ I legally changed my name to Par Reaper five years ago.

♂ The Statue of Liberty's pose was inspired by how people celebrate my golf game.

CHAPTER SEVEN

MOTHER NATURE FEARS ME!

The ability to survive is what separates the boys from the men. With a pocketknife, toothpick, and an empty beer bottle, a man can build a campsite complete with running water and a luxury gym. Men act with pure instinct when it comes to surviving in the wild. A man is not scared of the apocalypse or zombies because he already has a plan of action for any event. Lost on a deserted island, stuck in the jungle, or rappelling down Mount Everest without a harness, a man can survive it all.

Men, were not made for the concrete jungle, they were made for "surviving the suck" in the real jungle. When someone asks you about your survival skills don't settle for some lost indoors man answer. Always remember, **men don't just exist, they exaggerate**. Respond like this instead...

♂ Nature has a survival kit just in case I enter the woods.

♂ I can start a fire by whispering to the sticks.

♂ I can navigate the forest in complete darkness, using nothing but the stars and the disappointed voice of my father in my head.

♂ I have never had a sunburn because the sun fears hurting me.

44

♂ On a hot day I go swimming in lava to help me cool off.

SOS, More like LOL

Ask the common person what SOS means and you'll likely hear something like "save our ship", but that's not accurate. SOS is not an acronym. In 1905, the International Radiotelegraph Convention chose the three simple letters because it is simple to write and hard to confuse with other communications in Morse code. Now you can explain this to other men and be a know-it-all pompous jerk!

♂ I could carve a canoe out of a piece of granite.

♂ I filter my coffee through gravel.

♂ Never have I filtered my water while camping because bacteria fears me.

♂ I can sharpen my knife with my teeth.

♂ Thunderstorms fear me and go silent at my command.

♂ In Hawaii, I yelled at a volcano, and the volcano apologized for existing.

Life Hack It Up

Every survivalist has a dozen survival hacks up his sleeve and if you want to impress other dudes, then learn a couple. For example, a 9V Battery and steel wool is a great way to start a fire. If you also want to get a laugh, don't forget about sharing that tampons are great for stopping a bloody nose, act as kindling for a fire, and even may be used as a water filter in desperate times.

♂ I use a plastic spoon as a shovel and can move more dirt than a tractor.

♂ For hiking shoes, I wear two bear traps.

♂ The only toilet paper I use is tree bark.

♂ I can light a match 10 feet under the water, using my feet.

Hold it Right There

Getting lost in the woods may sound poetic, but it's a terrifying thought. Statistics show that 90% of people lost are eventually found. That means that 10% are never seen again. Here's a pro-tip... if you are ever lost in the woods, the best strategy is to stay in place and wait for help. Going on a walk about may sound like a great idea, but it's not!

♂ I can build a campfire by rubbing my left nut and right nut together.

♂ I once growled at a bear, and it went into the fetal position.

♂ I only play jump rope if a venomous snake is the rope.

♂ I am banned from zoos because I scare the animals into reverse evolution. They all crawl back into the swamp.

♂ I punched a glacier with my little finger and turned it into crushed ice.

Dip Your Stick?

There is nothing worse than needing to build a fire on the spot and finding a pocket full of wet matches. Fortunately, waterproof matches are not difficult to make. All you need is melted paraffin wax or clear nail polish. 10 out of 10 survivalists recommend dipping your stick before every camping trip.

♂ I reverse engineered fire to help cool down the cave I was sleeping in.

♂ I build fires so well that my smoke signals are seen from space.

♂ I can build a fire during a thunderstorm, with wet wood, and soggy matches.

♂ I can tap on a log and hear the moisture content.

♂ My favorite way to get a fire going is by rubbing my beard stubble on an oak tree.

Potty Mouth

Drinking urine is a survival technique that does work, but it comes with some risks. In a survival situation, a man does what he must do. Here is a pro-tip if you ever end up in a situation where pee is your best option for hydration, don't brag about it to your friends.

A Mouth Full of Advice: Keep the urine-drinking to yourself, both literally and metaphorically. We are all glad you survived but keep the "how" to yourself!

♂ I can build a campfire so impressive that the smoke can be seen from space.

♂ I use a multi-tool to open delivery packages.

♂ I can pitch a tent, roast a marshmallow, and start a fire all at the same time.

♂ With a 5-gallon bucket full of pine cones and duct tape, I can build a five-star hotel.

♂ I can feed a village with a couple of paperclips and a shoestring.

Berry Roulette – Mother Nature's Lottery

This is where "hungry" and "ready to die" violently collide. Roughly 20% of berries found in the forest are harmless. Likewise, 10% of berries contain deadly toxins.

Time Tested Wisdom: Be careful what you put in your mouth!

♂ At high noon, I can still navigate by the stars.

♂ With a few pieces of charcoal and an old t-shirt, I can filter water for a month.

♂ I never need tent stakes because my ego is a heavy enough anchor to the ground.

♂ My go-bag only has a mirror in it because I am all that I need to survive.

♂ I have never followed a path, but I have left many trails.

Nature's GPS

If you didn't take earlier advice and stay put when you are lost, then that's okay. The sun makes an excellent compass. Always remember that the sun rises in the east and sets in the west. Don't worry though, you will probably die somewhere in the middle!

♂ I can find water anywhere; that is why my camping friends call me the human canteen.

♂ I can turn a squirrel into a three-course meal.

♂ Only a novice outdoorsman needs a compass. I can navigate the woods with nothing more than a sniff of the air and instinct.

♂ Survival show experts call me before a new series is recorded to ask me for tips.

♂ Shopping centers buy the blueprints for the shelters I build in the woods.

Mr. Cactus is a Prick

In the movies, survival in the desert equates to the hero cutting open a cactus and a fresh stream of water starts flowing. The truth is that cacti are not just prickly to the touch, but they are also pricks about sharing their water. Several species of cacti are toxic to prevent animals from obtaining water from them. In a desert survival situation, you are better off finding shade, searching for water, or kissing your butt goodbye than you are to rely on a cactus for hydration.

CHAPTER EIGHT
TAMING BEARS & EATING NAILS

All men know that the smallest inconvenience is worthy of being retold as a tale of toughness. A tiny splinter? More like pulling a railroad spike out of our palm! Getting up early to go on a trail hike sounds more like sleep deprivation training for combat operations. Ask us about that "almost" fight we got into at the bar, and we will tell you how we fought a biker gang solo. Heaven forbid us to have a bruise because you will never hear the end of it. The saga of exaggerating our toughness echoes throughout a man's life.

As the philosopher A.R. Weston once said, "Chicks dig scars, bros fight in bars, and grit makes men into stars!" When someone asks you about your toughness don't settle for some flowery marshmallow reply. Always remember, **men don't just exist, they exaggerate**. Respond like this instead...

♂   Sleep is for the weak. I can recharge by intimidating the darkness.

♂   When I was born, I cut my own umbilical cord with my teeth.

♂   Last week I taught a lion to roar.

♂   My sandals are tied with braided steel.

♂ I wrestled fear and now it is afraid of me.

Stubbed Toe or War Story?

Proving toughness is not always easy, but with the right amount of embellishment, a clumsy moment, like stubbing a toe on the laundry bin your wife placed in front of the bed, can transcend into an epic saga of fighting through gunfire and shrapnel.

Bro-Tip: A man knows how to turn his poor depth perception into a heroic tale of manliness and valor.

♂ Trees shed their leaves prematurely when they see me approaching them.

♂ I sweat bullets and acid, literally.

♂ I snack on danger and feast on adversity.

♂ I refer to lions, tigers, and bears as the perfect petting zoo.

♂ I tell pain to take a number, and I never call back.

Mind Over Bladder

What does toughness look like? Fighting a lion? Pulling a splinter the size of a railroad spike out of your leg? That's child's play compared to needing to pee when you're 30 minutes into a 4-hour car trip. When your teeth start to float, don't panic. The toughest part of a man's body is his mind. Don't do mind over matter, try mind over bladder!

♂ A bowl of danger and cup of no regrets is how I start my morning routine.

♂ The dentist had to use a sledgehammer to take out my wisdom teeth.

♂ I can get blood from a stone.

♂ Grizzly bears convert to veganism when they see how inferior they are compared to me.

♂ I wrestled a moose in Canada and now it identifies as a deer.

Headlock Hero

The ability to explain and demonstrate different types of headlocks is the ultimate tough guy brag. Mastering and expanding your headlock arsenal will transform you into a legend. After all, headlocks are nothing more than an aggressive friendly hug.

Cave Dweller Protocol: A rear-naked-choke should never be done naked...

♂ I have never been bitten by a mosquito because they know better.

♂ I've never backed down from anything, unlike you.

♂ I am the first man to kill a tornado, and I did it for sport.

♂ All my cigars are lit with a blowtorch.

Grit as a Key Performance Indicator (KPI)

Exceeds Expectations	Relentless, Resolute, Steadfast
Meets Expectations	Reliable, Steady, Grounded
Needs Improvement	Unacceptable, Intolerable

♂ I had a dream that my nightmares were having dreams about me haunting them.

♂ The last can of whoop-ass I opened apologized to me.

♂ I sign my autograph by leaving bruises on my fans.

♂ I have broken several pieces of furniture by stubbing my toe.

♂ At the top of my to-do list is to make you feel weak every chance I get.

Man-gnificent Pain Tolerance

There are two things that play a role in a person's pain tolerance, genetics and will-power. If you want to boast about your ability to handle pain, boldly claim that your predisposition is to deal with high levels of pain and that mind over matter is your approach to agony. You were simply born rough, tough, and hard to bluff!

♂ The only real way to make coffee is to chew the bean and sip boiling water.

♂ When I cut my foot in the war, I stitched it up with razor wire.

♂ I hugged a cactus to help it toughen up and be less of a prick.

♂ The rock quarry hired me to crush granite with the power of my jawline.

♂ A grit level has not been invented for how rough I am, yet.

♂ When I go to the club, the bouncers ask me if they are on my list.

The Alpha-Male Equation

$$T = (P * S) + (R - F)$$

Toughness = (Pain * Sweat) + (Results – Failures)

♂ During puberty, my voice cracked... the foundations of the earth.

♂ My reflection filed a restraining order against me for being too intimidating.

♂ I catch fire ants in a bottle and use them to exfoliate my skin.

♂ I shave my neck hair with broken glass.

♂ The army issued me a butterknife, and I turned it into a bayonet.

♂ At my command, the rain turns to whiskey.

Old School Medieval Toughness

Did you know that back in the day, barbershops did more than cut hair? A good barber would perform tooth extractions, bloodletting, boil removal and other minor surgeries. There were no pain meds, no sterile bandages, just another day at the barbershop.

♂ I played chicken with a tank and won... twice.

♂ I squeeze lemon juice in my eyes because it tickles.

♂ I once hand-forged an axe by breaking a sword in half.

♂ My preferred bubble gum is a leather strap soaked in whiskey.

Truth Stretcher

This tip is simple. No matter what, never, ever, admit that you needed a stretcher or an ambulance. When you are explaining to your buddies what happened, the story must always end with you walking away on your own with no help.

♂ My skin is so thick that a tattooist must use a box cutter and spray paint to give me a tattoo. It still fades away after 24 hours.

♂ When life hands me lemons, I ask for a shot of tequila.

♂ I have more testosterone than a bull stampede in a cage full of lions.

♂ I could steal honey from a bear, and it would apologize to me.

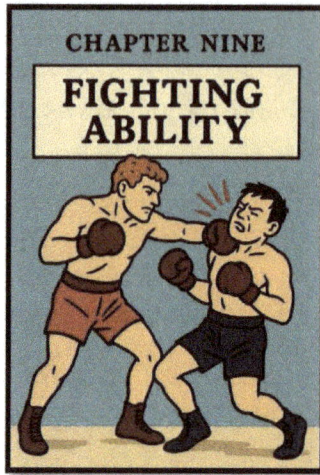

CHAPTER NINE

FIGHTING ABILITY

It is uncommon to meet a man who doesn't think he would obviously win a fight even though he has never thrown a punch, or that his "battle stance" looks like a toddler guarding the last chicken nugget before his big sister snatches it. Ask any man and you will hear stories about the martial arts classes he took in elementary school. Sure, he quit after two weeks, but he did earn his yellow belt and is still a lethal weapon.

Bragging about brawling and being scrappy is essential for a man. Pretending we are always ready to rumble is manlier than a lumberjack slaying a dragon. When someone asks you about your fighting ability, don't settle for some pillow-fisted answer. Always remember, **men don't just exist, they exaggerate**. Respond like this instead...

♂ I started a fight with a guy, and he apologized for something he didn't even do.

♂ In a fight, I always politely ask if my opponent prefers to tap or be knocked out.

♂ I can turn a large tree into mulch with a couple of kicks.

♂ I can elbow a boulder and turn it into a pebble.

Speak Slow and Carry a Big.... Voice!

We are all born with three innate fears. The fear of falling, the fear of complete darkness, and the fear of loud noises. The startle reflex is real, and it can be used in your favor during a fight. Yell, roar, snarl, growl, and bellow to intimidate your opponent. Worst case, if it doesn't work and you get stomped into the ground, at least you burst his ear drums.

♂ I shadow boxed my own shadow and turned it into daylight.

♂ I could punch a mirror and it would self-reflect on its life choices.

♂ I can uppercut rain clouds and convert them into fog.

♂ My Thanksgiving turkey is carved using only karate chops.

♂ I can slap winter into summer and kick spring into fall.

Fake the Funk

There is an ancient proverb that says, "Those that can't do, teach." Leading up to a fight, it's more like, "Those that can't fight, pretend." Call it bluffing, feigning, or posturing, but it may save your life. If the other guy is not confident in his fighting ability, then putting on a good pseudo act of fighting bravado may convince your opponent to leave you alone.

♂ My punching bag starts to cry when I train.

♂ I can fight city hall and win.

♂ I could turn a mountain into a valley with a single kick.

♂ I could roast a marshmallow using the heat from my punch.

♂ I keep a journal to track all the fights I have lost. I've never needed to write anything.

♂ I once blocked a punch with my shadow and the other guy's shadow flinched.

♂ I punched a guy into a flashback.

Tiny, But Mighty

Are you a puny fellow that everyone underestimates in a fight? When other men look at you, do they assume you're a wimp because of your tiny stature? Well, don't despair. The Mantis Shrimp feels your pain, but he doesn't cry about it because he is too busy breaking jaws. Remind your buddies that pound for pound you carry a heavy hit, like the Mantis Shrimp.

♂ I never fight dirty because dirty is too clean of a fighting style for me.

♂ I have ducked a punch so fast that I saw my childhood flash before my eyes.

♂ I never get into fights because my reputation negotiates the other guy's surrender when I walk into the room.

♂ When I started martial arts training, I immediately challenged the sensei to a fight, now I am his teacher.

Quicker Than Science

According to science, if that means anything these days, the fastest possible human reaction time to stimulus is 101 milliseconds. That is as fast as a blink. Want to impress your pals regarding your catlike reflexes? Tell them that your reaction capabilities are measured in nanoseconds.

♂ I once got into a bar fight with three guys and used pool noodles as a weapon. I won.

♂ I block punches before my opponent thinks about throwing them.

♂ I can dodge a punch, laugh, counter, and take a swig of my drink before my opponent finishes his swing.

♂ At my last physical, the doctor said I didn't have reflexes, but that I was born with pre-flexes.

♂ My kicks are banned in six countries and in three alternate universes.

♂ My kick can change the direction of the wind.

♂ I could fold you like a fitted sheet at a five-star hotel.

The Octopus Swinger

The universal rule in fighting is that you can't win by freezing and you also won't win by flailing. Winning a fight is 60% defense and 40% offense. What this means is that you don't want your fighting style to resemble a drunken octopus. Protect your face. Swing when opportunity presents itself. Stick and move!

♂ I could punch you into next week and get there before your body hits the floor.

♂ My punches don't make people bleed, they rearrange their DNA.

♂ I beat this guy so bad his grandkids will walk with a limp.

♂ I backhanded this guy so hard his brain went into airplane modc.

Know Your Martial Arts

Martial Art	Origin	Style
Karate	Japan	Strikes (punches, kicks, discipline)
Taekwondo	Korea	Dynamic high kicks, Olympic sport
Judo	Japan	Throws, grappling, submissions
Brazilian Jiu-Jitsu	Brazil	Ground fighting, submissions
Boxing (Modern)	England	Punching, striking
Muay Thai	Thailand	Striking with fists, elbows, knees, shins
Kung Fu	China	Varied traditions (Shaolin, Wing Chun, etc.)
Wrestling	Greece	Grappling, takedowns, control
Krav Maga	Israel	Self-defense, military efficiency
Aikido	Japan	Redirecting energy, locks, throws

♂ My fighting skills are measured with poetic precision, even Shakespeare would ask for lessons.

♂ I will bury you so deep into the curb that your kids will be born in the sewer.

♂ I pretended to throw a punch and the other guy's shadow flinched.

♂ I could rearrange your jaw and liberal arts majors will call it a modern work of art.

♂ I am such a good fighter I could beat you into an identity crisis.

Untrained vs. Trained vs. You

Category	Punching Power (LBF)
Untrained	100
Trained	300
Elite Fighters	1000+
Men Reading This Book	2000+

Disclaimer: Values not verified, but we all have faith in you!

♂ I punched a breaker box and killed the power for the whole town.

♂ The judge ordered me to tattoo warning labels on my fists.

♂ I once stomped a bug into a fossil.

♂ I punched a piece of charcoal and it instantly turned into a diamond.

♂ Global warming didn't start with fossil fuels, it started with me roundhouse kicking an iceberg.

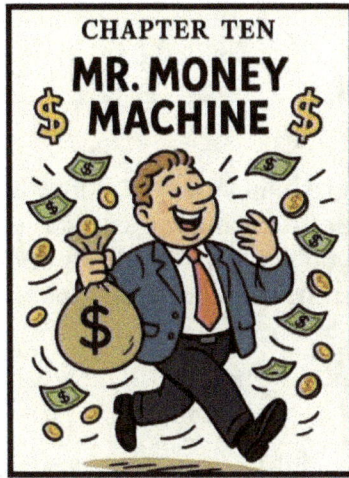

CHAPTER TEN

MR. MONEY MACHINE

Investments, stock options, private equity lines, hedge funds, venture capital, IPO, ROI, liquidity, and offshore accounts are but a few of the many terms the financially savvy man lives by. Men love turning their earnings into egomaniac style rants about their economic genius. Our inflated optimism and unrealistic expectations regarding returns comes with the best of intentions. To a man, money is a symbol of pride, success, confidence, and hope for a better tomorrow.

Being rich is not easy, but someone's got to do it! When someone asks you about your wealth don't settle for a broke financially challenged answer. Always remember, **men don't just exist, they exaggerate**. Respond like this instead...

♂ I am so well off that last year the bank asked me for a loan.

♂ I stopped carrying cash and now all I have in my wallet is influence.

♂ I dropped my wallet and the economy crashed.

♂ I made it rain at the club one night and I saw Noah building another ark in the parking lot.

♂ I sent so much money in the mail, I accidentally bought the post office.

Baller on a Budget

Here is a unique life hack to help you save money. Refill your empty ketchup bottles in fast food restaurants using the self-serve condiment pump. Over the course of five years, you will save hundreds of dollars, and all your friends will disassociate from you, too. Win-win!

♂ I have so much money that my tissue box is a stack of $100 bills.

♂ Some men shake hands to complete a transaction, all I do is blink and the money enters my bank account.

♂ I am so loaded that the water in my sauna is heated with passive income.

♂ I have so much money that I bought my financial advisor a financial advisor for Christmas.

♂ I audited the IRS last year for fun.

Briefcase Full of Dough

In movies, bad guys fill a briefcase with cash, but how much money would "actually" fit? A standard case can hold roughly 9,000 individual bills stacked in 18 bundles of 500 bills. If using 20-dollar increments, it means the baddies are offering about $180,000. A random fact to exaggerate your knowledge of money!

♂ I got my dog a trust fund last year, a private plane, a yacht, and a lawyer.

♂ I have more zeros in my portfolio than your dating history.

♂ I wipe with hundreds because twenties make my cheeks chafe.

A Real Golden Shower

Don't worry, no one is getting peed on! Let's talk about the cost of installing a real golden shower in your house. Suppose you have a 120 Sq Ft shower (floors + walls). Using 24k gold laminate, the approximate cost is upwards of $200k. Paying someone to spritz urine on you is probably cheaper, however.

♂ My wallet has its own zip code and post office.

♂ The change under my driver's seat is enough to buy a small country and still leave a tip.

♂ I am so rich the bank ran out of zeros at the end of my account.

♂ My bank statements are only visible in panoramic mode.

KWD vs USD

Wealthy men know currency exchange rates. Did you know the Kuwaiti Dollar is worth 3.25 U.S. dollars. If you didn't know that what does it say about your financial status?

♂ My idea of being broke is having to borrow my neighbor's jet for a weekend getaway to my private island.

♂ My shadow pays more taxes than you.

♂ I once paid for an extinct animal species to be brought back for a luxury jacket, wallet, and boots to be made.

♂ The bank measures my credit limit using light-years.

♂ People refer to my pockets as the Mariana Trench.

Heli-Cash-Ter

Owning a helicopter is the ultimate rich guy brag. The good news is that anyone can own one. All you need is a million dollars plus annual operating costs. You can make quick trips for brunch, casual commutes to the beach, and pick up super models... What's holding you back?

♂ I refer to Ft. Knox as my own personal piggy bank.

♂ The bank approves million-dollar loans based solely on the contents of my safe deposit box.

♂ I bought an ocean last year to park my yacht.

♂ I am the first man to yawn and subsequently raise the stock price at my company.

♂ I donate my pocket lint for charity and write it off on my taxes.

Sultan Style

Do you collect cars? At what point does a man go from having a few vehicles to being a legit car collector? The answer is highly subjective, but there is no disputing the fact that the world's largest car collection belongs to the Sultan of Brunei. His collection is comprised of 7,000 vehicles and is worth a little over 5 billion dollars.

♂ I am the first man to order take out and buy the restaurant at the same time.

♂ My Wi-Fi router is named "buy-everything" and the password is "wire-transfer!"

♂ I lost the key to my sports car in the couch, so I bought a new sports car.

♂ My wallet wouldn't close so I installed utility hinges and a deadbolt lock.

♂ I bought the Great Pyramid of Giza in Egypt and am renovating it into a game room.

♂ I have more valuables in my junk drawer than a bank vault does.

Just the Tip

If a man leaves a big tip and no one is around to see it, did it happen? Researchers are still trying to answer this question, but there is certainly a connection between big tips and ego. Sure, rewarding good service is the foundation, but ego is the cornerstone. Here is how to scientifically assess your tipping protocols:

Tip Percentage	Our Perception
0% – 5%	You're a Jerk!
6% – 10%	Cheapskate
11% – 24%	Good Chap
25% +	Either Overly Generous or an Idiot

♂ I once lost a house early in a high stakes poker game and left owning a sovereign nation.

♂ My dog-tags are two gold bars with my name carved into them and hanging around my neck.

Hypothetically Speaking

These are the questions that keep us all up at night. Let's say that the Great Pyramid of Giza were put up for sale, how much would it cost to buy? If you consider the modern build replacement cost (material + labor) and add yearly revenue generation from tourism, then you could ball park it easily. Per experts in napkin math, if you carry the one, and don't forget to apply the Pythagorean theorem, it will cost approximately 11.2 billion USD to purchase the thing.

I have more dollars in my bank account than the beach has grains of sand.

CHAPTER ELEVEN

ATHLETIC DEMIGOD

Bragging about our athletic ability is not a new phenomenon for men. When it comes to boasting, there is nothing more instinctual than telling other guys about our glory days of playing high school football or making the varsity basketball team when we were only in the 8th grade. If it weren't for that sprained ankle in college, we would still be playing in the pros and not stuck at a boring desk job. Our legendary stories about god-like athletic abilities are a staple of every man worth his salt.

A great aphorism declares, "Boys play games, but men play sports." When someone asks you about your athletic ability, don't settle for some flimsy modest answer. Always remember, **men don't just exist, they exaggerate**. Respond like this instead...

♂ I am so fast that during a relay race, I once lapped myself, twice.

♂ I am the only human to ever dunk on a giraffe during a basketball game.

♂ I could outrun a cheetah with a whole leg cast and crutches.

♂ Laundromats pay me to let customers iron their clothes on my stomach.

♂ My arm is so strong I once threw a plastic ball over Mt. Everest.

♂ The mirrors in the gym are not big enough to reflect my greatness.

How does your sprint speed compare to the average person?

Age	100 Meter Time	Speed (MPH)
15–19	13–14 sec	17–19 mph
20–24	12–13 sec	18–20 mph
25–29	12–13.5 sec	17–19 mph
30–34	13–14 sec	16–18 mph
35–39	13.5–14.5 sec	15–17 mph
40–44	14–15 sec	15–16 mph
45–49	15–16 sec	14–15 mph
50–59	16–18 sec	12–14 mph
60–69	18–20 sec	11–12 mph
70+	20+ sec	9–10 mph

♂ I won MVP in a baseball game that was canceled due to lightning.

♂ Treadmills scream and the bench press moans when I enter the gym.

♂ My vertical is so high that space programs study me for anti-gravity research.

♂ When I flex in the gym, the lights flicker, and personal trainers run out of the building, weeping.

♂ I could do a backflip over the Grand Canyon with a cinder block tied to my boots.

Let's Get Vertical, Vertical!

People talk, but numbers scream. Nothing shouts "athlete" like a man with a solid vertical jump. So, what is a good height for a vertical? An average guy can jump anywhere from 18 to 20 inches high. The elite athlete can nearly double that height. If you want to impress, then at minimum you need a 28" vertical!

♂ My sweat instantly turns into bourbon.

♂ I can do more pushups than you, with no hands.

♂ My baseball swing is so hot it leaves the ball asking for a cigarette.

♂ I have never stolen a base, but I do seduce the plate into letting me come early.

♂ My warm up swing turns more heads than a super model.

Omni-Athlete

Do you play a lot of sports? Have you played them all? Think about this before you commit to your answer. There are roughly 200 recognized sports worldwide. If you dedicated 3 months to learning, practicing, and playing every sport, it would take you 50 years to say you played them all.

♂ I hit a baseball the same way I take my coffee... fast, strong, and guaranteed to energize.

♂ I have spent more time in the penalty box than you have spent in marriage counseling.

♂ People say that "You miss 100% of the shots you never take", unless you are me.

♂ I threw a spiral pass so well that the football started to undress in the air.

Trick Question

What is the better sport, Bodybuilding or High Intensity Functional Training?

Hint: High Intensity Functional Training is not a real sport.

♂ I wear two helmets in a football game, one for my head, and the other for my ego.

♂ I hear moaning in the crowd when I throw a stiff arm in the game.

♂ I pull log trucks out of the ditch as a warm up exercise.

♂ I run the football like I am trying to avoid paying taxes.

Bowlers: The Real Athletes

It's time we put this debate to rest. Football players hit each other, soccer players kick a ball, and basketball players dunk. The final evolution of athletic performance is not found on a field or track, it's found under the fluorescent lights of the bowling lane. Bowling requires precision, power, and endurance. Any athlete that can down nachos, a chili dog, and pitcher of beer and then dominate a sport is the real hero!

♂ My bowling ball doesn't roll, it seduces the lane to drop its pins.

♂ I treat my spares in bowling better than you care for your family.

♂ I can burn more calories in my warm up than most can during a marathon.

♂ The energy generated from my stationary bike rivals a nuclear power plant.

♂ The last stopwatch I used to time my 40 broke due to whiplash.

Run Till You Die? No Thank You!

The legend of Pheidippides running 25 miles after the Battle of Marathon in 490 B.C. to announce victory over the Persians and then dying from exhaustion is a mix of myth and truth. The moral of the story, however, is not. God did not intend for anyone to run that far. Men were designed to lift heavy weights and flex in front of the mirror.

♂ At the end of my 100-yard dash I use a fire extinguisher on my shoes because my sprints create flames.

♂ People refer to my vertical jump as "gravity defying!"

♂ Gyms collect and sell my sweat as a legal performance enhancer.

♂ It is common for competitors to quit the race before it begins when they see me line up at the start.

♂ I once hit a baseball into the sky and it came back to earth the next year as a meteorite.

Scared to Squat

Question: Why did the endurance athlete leave the gym?

Answer: He remembered it was leg day!

♂ I could skip leg days for the rest of my life and my quads would still be bigger than yours, but I would never skip leg days.

♂ I once jumped rope into another dimension because I was going too fast.

♂ The IRS made me list my body fat percentage as an asset.

♂ My cardio routine is chasing lightning bolts before they hit the ground.

♂ I could catch a falling star with my bare hands and punt it back into space.

Vertical Ambition

When it comes to the ultimate test of athletic ability, there are no activities that rival climbing Mount Everest. Lack of oxygen, extreme altitudes, icefalls, and sleep deprivation are only a few of the perils the mountain holds. This is why claiming that you are prepping to climb Everest is the ultimate exaggeration for a man. Refer to your gym as basecamp, the stairs as altitude ascents, and post cryptic messages about your training on social media. #EverestLetsGo

♂ I once swam up a waterfall for fun.

♂ I could catch a meteor and throw it across the ocean.

♂ I can run so far and fast that I can catch tomorrow.

♂ My weight vest for ruck marching is a boulder.

♂ I could swim through lava and not get burned.

Surprise Burpees

Do you want to be admired for your athletic abilities? Do you love fitness? Then welcome to **Surprise Burpees**. Here is how it works... When you are in public, preferably around strangers, knock out a set of burpees. It works best if you count the repetitions out loud. This way, everyone will know you are committed to fitness and think how amazing you are and wish they were you. Try this out and I guarantee you will get noticed!

♂ I could power walk across the ocean without getting wet.

♂ Not only can I outrun my past, but I can lap it.

♂ I could outrun a mudslide, uphill, without shoes or legs.

CHAPTER TWELVE

BREW BRAGGING BRAVADO

If the ability to consume large quantities of adult beverages were an Olympic event, then most men exceeding 21-year-olds would be an elite athlete. It is common speak in the world of men to exaggerate their drinking ability with expressions like, "I could drink anyone under the table", "I have a hollow leg", and "I drink like a fish." Keg stands, shot-gunning drinks from a plastic funnel, and multiple rounds of beer pong are a rite of passage into adulthood. The only thing more inflated than the number of drinks we boast about is our ego.

Like daddy always slurred when he stumbled inside, "I'm not as think as you drunk I am!" When someone questions your drinking capabilities, don't settle for some sober clear-eyed answer. Always remember, **men don't just exist, they exaggerate**. Respond like this instead...

♂ I can drink so much beer that my blood type is now IPA – Positive.

♂ I can drink a flaming shot while it is still on fire.

♂ The hospital uses whiskey in the I.V. to keep me hydrated.

♂ I once drank so much that I didn't black out, but I time traveled.

♂ When I play beer pong, I fill the cups with gasoline, and I still win every time.

Beer Before Liquor, Never Sicker

The Germans say it best...

> *"Bier auf Wein, das lass sein, Wein auf Bier, das rat' ich dir."*
>
> "Beer after wine, leave it be, wine after beer, I recommend it to thee."

Amen!

♂ When I do cardio, my sweat is 90 proof whiskey.

♂ The best mouthwash is moonshine.

♂ I once drank a cocktail so strong that it had to register as a weapon of mass destruction.

♂ Russian sailors wish they could drink as much vodka as me.

♂ I can pop a champagne cork with no hands. The cork pops out of respect for me.

Science is a Buzzkill

If water hydrates you, and hydration is good, and beer is 90% water, then wouldn't it be healthy to drink more beer? Every frat boy likely nodded and agreed. Beer dehydrates you because alcohol blocks ADH, a chemical that helps your kidneys retain water. You don't just pee more when you drink alcohol, but your body is flushing water that would normally be retained. Bummer, I know!

♂ My liver is currently writing its first memoir titled "More Whiskey, Please!"

♂ I am known for shutting down wine tastings before they even start.

♂ I play drinking games using a fishbowl full of rum as my shot glass.

♂ The police department gave me an award for highest score on the breathalyzer.

♂ I once drank a margarita the size of an Olympic pool.

♂ Champagne bottles pop when I walk into the room.

Your Liver is Hot... Literally

Your liver is a powerful and incredible organ. When you drink alcohol, part of the warmth resonating from your soul is due to a process called oxidation happening in your liver. Your liver is literally heating up to process the alcohol. Combine this with blood vessel dilation and you become one hot sexy beast. Alright, maybe not the sexy part, but you get the point!

♂ I shotgun a beer so fast that the can apologizes for slowing me down.

♂ The last breathalyzer I took read, "You again?"

♂ My whiskey collection has its own zip code.

♂ I drink shots so fast that the glass gets whiplash.

♂ My liver has its own gym membership.

I'm Hung Like a Japanese Shot Glass

Did you know not all countries have the same size shot glass?

Country	Standard Shot Glass
United States	1.5 Ounce
Canada	1.25 Ounce
United Kingdom	1 Ounce
Japan	2 Ounce
Mexico	1.7 Ounce
Australia	1 Ounce

♂ I have never blacked out from drinking; the night just couldn't keep up with me.

♂ I played on both sides of a beer pong table at the same time and still won.

♂ Bartenders always ask me what is on tap.

♂ My bar tab has its own savings account and 401k plan.

♂ The alcohol level of my spit has been labeled a wildfire hazard.

Spin to Win...

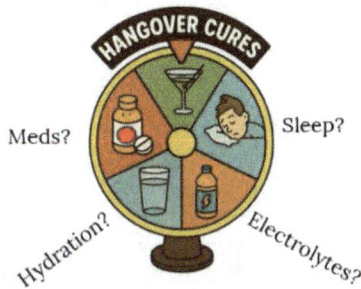

♂ My beer stays chill all night out of respect for my drinking abilities.

♂ I refer to blacking out as entering stealth mode.

♂ I drank moonshine so strong that my soul flinched.

♂ Tequila doesn't make me dance, but I make tequila perform.

♂ Bars won't officially start happy hour until I arrive and start drinking.

♂ The Governor of Kentucky sent me a thank you card for drinking so much bourbon.

♂ Scholars draft their doctoral dissertations regarding their observations of my extraordinary drinking capabilities.

Solo Kegger

A full-sized keg holds 15.5 gallons of beer. That is 165 cans of beer. Let's say you wanted to finish a keg by yourself. If you drank 5 beers a day, it would take you over a month to finish the whole thing solo. It would be a great month, though!

♂ I can drink a flaming shot and roast a marshmallow with my breath.

♂ My last hangover begged me for mercy.

♂ My liver has an official fan page, and I am the president.

♂ I once blew a breathalyzer so high that the cop gave me two thumbs up.

Know Your Beers!

Beer Style	Origin	A.R. Opinions
Pilsner	Czech Republic	Crisp, golden lager.
IPA	England	Hoppy and strong.
Stout	Ireland	Dark and heavy.
Porter	England	Rich and malty.
Lager	Germany	Clean.
Hefeweizen	Germany	Cloudy wheat beer.
Saison	Belgium	Fruity and spicy.
Lambic	Belgium	Sour and funky.
Pale Ale	England	Malty and hoppy.
Barleywine	England	Strong and malty.
Bock	Germany	Strong, dark and malty.
Gose	Germany	Sour wheat.
Pale Lager	United States	Lighter taste.

CHAPTER THIRTEEN

MUSCLES DON'T LIE

Exaggerating size, strength, and muscle tone is a manly tradition older than popping pimples on our back. Cave dwellers likely strutted back into the cave after hunting a mammoth, climbed on top of a boulder, and flexed like professional wrestlers. The men cheered, the women dripped with perspiration, and young guys dreamt of one day when they too could be a ripped stud. Today, not much has changed, except now the mammoth is a soy latte, the boulder is social media, and muscles are accomplished through camera filters. Regardless, the principle of the matter remains the same... men exist to exaggerate, and muscularity is at the top of the list.

When someone questions your muscles and strength, don't settle for some featherweight weak answer. Always remember, **men don't just exist, they exaggerate**. Respond like this instead...

♂ Only the weak need two trips. I can carry all my groceries in one trip, every time, with one hand, in a cast.

♂ I can mix a wheelbarrow full of concrete using my pinky finger.

♂ I once kayaked on a river and the power of my paddling reversed the current.

♂ When my wife wants to clean under the couch, I military press it over my head while she vacuums.

♂ One of my hobbies is catching falling trees in the forest and then replanting them by hand.

The Bro-Code of Bench Pressing

While there is no official rule book for the gym, there is a universal principle that all men live by. A man should be able to bench press his own bodyweight! Try to think of benching your own body weight as a badge of entry level strength. The reality is that a man bench pressing his own weight is not impressive in Bro-Land. It should serve only as a launching point for strength and not as a destination.

♂ I can tie a knot in a steel cable using only my mouth.

♂ I can hammer coal into diamonds.

♂ My grip strength can turn a diamond back into coal.

♂ I can bend a wrench into a horseshoe.

♂ My hugs are known to crack ribs.

Do You Even Pull Up?

Let's talk about the basics of physical fitness for a moment. Please do some honest self-reflection! How many pull-ups can you do? It is estimated that less than 5% of men can do multiple pull-ups and many couldn't do a single pull up. Unacceptable! Master the basics first, push-ups, pull-ups, sit-ups, and a two-mile run.

♂ I can open a pickle jar with two fingers.

♂ I can bench press your mom with one arm.

♂ My handshake has been declared a weapon of mass destruction by the U.N.

♂   I can carry your emotional baggage and my luggage at the same time.

Got Veins?

When leanness and muscularity collide, something magical happens. All men know there is a difference between being called bulky vs. declared shredded. There is an old poem, made up just now by yours truly, that declares, "When your fat goes, and your muscles grow, then your veins will show!" The secret to vascularity is simple. You already have all the veins, they are hiding under a layer of fat. Eliminate fat, increase muscle size, and you will have that ripped appearance you desire.

♂   Supplement companies buy my blood and add it to their products to make them more anabolic.

♂   Statues of Ancient Greek warriors stop and take pictures of me.

♂   I can crack a walnut with my glutes.

♂   I don't skip leg days, but leg days skip me.

Somatotype Hype

In case you don't remember 6th grade P.E. class, somatotypes is when the gym teacher holds up a sign of three body types which are ectomorphs, mesomorphs, and endomorphs. To refresh your memory, the Ectos are the hard gainers, the Endos all play offensive line, and the Mesos are Greek gods that everyone else worships.

♂   I could iron your mom's clothes with my biceps and body heat.

♂   I stand on my front porch once a month and flex to keep my property value high.

♂   I wear a full suit of body armor to protect others from my muscles.

♂ I stop counting reps when I blackout and then wake up with bigger muscles.

♂ The airlines charge me for an extra bag when they see my traps.

Butt Cheeks of Steel

Philosophers commonly say that "behind every great lifter is a gluteus maximus doing all the work!" So, they don't really say that, but it is a true statement that from a size and power perspective, the strongest muscle on your body is your butt!

♂ My biceps and pecs are impressive, but I can also flex my eyebrows.

♂ I once cracked a bowling ball with a fist bump.

♂ I squat so deep that my butthole winks at the earth's core.

♂ My lats are so wide it is illegal for me to turn around in crowded spaces.

♂ I don't sweat, but I do secrete anabolic dominance.

Perception is Reality

Bicep Size (Flexed)	Perception
10 inches or smaller	Toothpicks - LOL
11 - 12 inches	Training Wheels for Muscles
13 - 15 inches	Nothing to Write Home About
16 - 17 inches	Swole
18 inches or bigger	Welcome to the Gun Show

♂ I was the first man to arm wrestle gravity and I won.

♂ The stretchmarks on my biceps have started to form stretch marks from all the gains.

♂ My brain may be emotionally stunted, but my quads and calves are naturally superior.

♂ My earlobes are stronger than your legs.

♂ My pre-workout is a blend of gasoline, TNT, and daddy issues.

The Manly Guide to Bodyfat Percentages

Percentage	Description	
3-5%	Anatomy chart with abs so sharp they could julienne fries	
6-9%	Greek statue with visible veins and zero joy	
10-12%	Fit guy at the beach – defined but human	
13-15%	Soft outline of abs – "they're there, just resting"	
20-24%	Dad strength unlocked	
25-29%	Winter bulking year-round	
30%+	Built for comfort, not for speed	

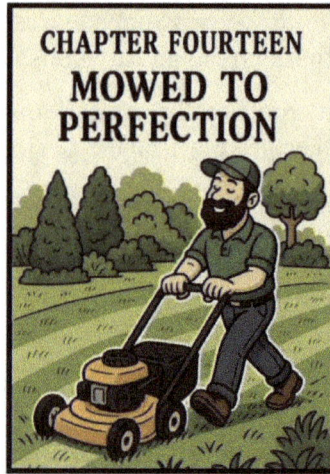

CHAPTER FOURTEEN
MOWED TO PERFECTION

The connection between a man and his lawn is undeniable. Every blade of grass is a little green trophy in the battlefield of keeping up with the Jones'. Tilling, sowing seeds, raking, dethatching, aerating, and mowing are a few activities in the arsenal of lawn care protocol. A man's lawn tells a story about his pride and self-worth. Strangers driving by may mistake the landscaping for an amateur botanical garden. Of course, the reality is often that we occasionally fertilize, do a little edging, and try our best to keep the crabgrass from taking over.

When someone asks you about your lawn, don't settle for a weedy, patchy reply. Always remember, **men don't just exist, they exaggerate**. Respond like this instead...

♂   My lawn is nicer than yours and all I use for fertilizer is my own urine.

♂   I never mow my lawn, I conduct it like a symphony, and I am the orchestra maestro.

♂   When I edge my yard, the men on my street stop and salute.

♂   My hedges are trimmed so precisely that the pentagon created battle plans based on them.

80

♂ The weeds that grow in my yard are better than the flowers that grow in yours.

Straight Outta Compost

An easy manly brag for lawn care is having your own compost pile. Let's talk about creating the perfect diet for your compost pile. Adding green yard waste like grass clippings will increase nitrogen while adding brown waste, such as dead leaves, increases carbon. Here is a free tip: If compost is stinky, then you are feeding it too many greens. If compost is too dry, then you are not providing enough greens.

Pro-Tip: For best results, use 1-part green waste for every 3-part brown waste.

♂ I whisper sweet nothings to my lawn and it grows in perfect stripes.

♂ The HOA in my subdivision fined me for having too high of standards for my yard.

♂ My lawn is so peaceful you can hear photosynthesis happening.

♂ Bedding factories buy the grass clippings from my yard and use them to fill their mattresses.

♂ Barbers ask me for a tutorial after they see how well I trim my bushes.

Ripping and Tearing

Imagine sitting down in the barber's chair and the barber starts buzzing your hair with a trimmer with a dull blade. With every pass, hair is not cut but ripped from your skull. That's not a haircut, it's torture. Mowing a yard with a dull lawnmower blade is not mowing, it's mangling. Causing unnecessary stress on your grass invites weeds because the grass takes longer to heal from you butchering it.

Mow Like a Pro: At minimum, sharpen mower blades twice each season and replace your blade every 3 years.

♂   Why does the sun rise? To see my lawn glisten!

♂   At the end of a rainbow you won't find gold, just my beautiful lawn.

♂   My mowing stripes are smoother than whiskey and straighter than a plumb line.

♂   I sell the grass clippings from my yard to be used as luxury pillow filling.

♂   When I water my yard, I hear the soil whisper, "Thank you, daddy!"

Weed it and Weep

The war on weeds is an annual battle that all men must endure. Here are three tips to help you win in hand-to-weed combat.

I.   Focus on growing a healthy, well-fed lawn and the weeds will struggle to prosper.

II. Strike hard and strike often when defending your yard against weeds. Pull weeds by the root and don't wait for them to mature.

III. Use herbicides in the spring and fall. Be consistent.

♂   People call me the neurosurgeon of dethatching a lawn because of my meticulousness.

♂   My trees start pruning themselves when I open the shed door.

♂   Remember to take off your shoes before you walk on my lawn.

♂   Construction companies use my lawn to fine tune their leveling tools.

♂ You could eat soup out of my bird bath, it's that clean!

Go Mulch Yourself

The instinct to cover dirt is a primal predisposition. In ancient times, farmers would recycle straw, leaves, animal dung, and even old pottery to cover the soil. Fast forward several thousands of years, and mulching around trees, walkways, and flower gardens is alive and well. Mulching is not yard work, it is an outward expression of manliness.

♂ The koi in my pond fill out an application to be part of my landscaping.

♂ Squirrels sign a guest book before climbing my trees.

♂ I receive weekly requests to rent my back yard for extravagant weddings.

♂ I arrange all the flowers in my garden in alphabetical order.

♂ There is a waiting list for hummingbirds to visit my flowerbeds.

Moist?

Weeds need brute force, but a lawn needs loving tenderness. A yard needs hydration the same way men need coffee in the morning. The secret to a healthy yard is the right amount of moisture. Too little, and grass withers. Too much, and your lawn is a swamp. A man knows how to keep things perfectly moist.

♂ I only feed my lawn deionized water that originated from a glacier.

♂ Landscapers park in front of my lawn to take selfies.

♂ The definition of "perfection" is based on the pictures of my front yard.

♂ Geometry teachers take their students on field trips to my garden to teach them about symmetry.

Stripe, Stripe, Baby!

Whether you call it grass bending, pattern mowing, or lawn sex appeal, the art form of striping a yard has been practiced for ages. European aristocrats had their landscapers use heavy rolling pins pulled behind horses to bend the grass in a line pattern.

Budget Friendly Tip: You can create the same affluent appearance with a PVC pipe filled with sand and a couple of zip ties attached to your push mower.

♂ People from Ireland travel to see my lawn and refer to it as the *real* emerald isle.

♂ A 12-point buck approached the edge of my lawn, bowed, and shed his antlers to pay respect.

♂ Realtors send me offers to purchase my lawn, not the house, the lawn.

♂ I play Mozart music to my lawn at night because I want it to relax in perfect harmony.

Every Man Wants to Spread a Little Seed...

But what is the best seed to spread?

U.S. Region	Best Option
Northeast	Kentucky Bluegrass
Northwest	Perennial Ryegrass
Southeast	Bermuda Grass
Southwest	Buffalograss
Midwest	Tall Fescue

CHAPTER FIFTEEN
YOU FOLLOW, I LEAD

Respect is not given, it is earned. When a man talks about his leadership skills, you may confuse him as the reincarnate Caesar. Vision, mission statements, mottos, slogans, and little bits of wisdom are only a few attributes of a true leader. Men consider their ability to lead as sacred. A true leader doesn't need to yell, "Take the hill", because his followers are already halfway to the top dominating the competition. It's not about desiring power or prestige, it's about work ethic, drive, tenacity, honor, and integrity.

When someone asks you about your leadership skills, don't settle for some unimpressive, indecisive answer. Always remember, **men don't just exist, they exaggerate**. Respond like this instead...

♂ I never follow trends, but they sure follow me.

♂ People call me the compass of leadership because my way is always right.

♂ I once attended a leadership conference where I was the only speaker, and I still had to take notes.

♂ At work I delegate to the CEO, CFO, and COO, because they need a leader to tell them what to do.

♂ My shadow is a better leader than you and better looking.

Humor Box

We have all heard the typical attributes of a good leader. Let's see... listen, treat people with respect, be fair, and throw pizza parties on Fridays to keep employees from complaining too much. One trait that doesn't get enough love is the importance of humor.

Leadership Advice: Be the funniest leader you can be. If your staff howls that you took it too far, that's okay. Feel free to crack another joke knowing that H.R. stands for the department of "Human Ridiculousness."

♂ I can start a meeting with a smile and end it with a blink.

♂ My motivational speeches accidentally ignite revolutions.

♂ People create their own leadership blueprints from me sharing the dreams I had the night before.

♂ I herd cats and then teach them to march in unison.

♂ I could burp in a corporate meeting and my peers would take notes.

LPE, You Need All Three!

The best way to exaggerate your leadership ability starts with how your approach LPE...

Lead With...	Classic Definition	A.R. Translation
Logos	Lead with logic, reasoning, facts, and evidence, persuading others through the power of your brain!	Lead with your brain. What does the data tell you?
Pathos	Lead with empathy and storytelling, persuading others through the power of your heart.	Lead with your heart and genuinely care about others.
Ethos	Lead with integrity and honor, persuading others through trustworthiness.	Lead with ethics. Don't be a dirtbag!

♂ I am so strategic I accidentally won a chess match that I wasn't even playing.

♂ Employees write their notes in bold when they are listening to me present in meetings.

♂ Employees refer to me as both their leader and their life coach.

♂ HR keeps a file detailing my leadership prestige, initiative, and charisma.

♂ I don't give feedback, I issue clarity and precision.

♂ My meeting agendas are referred to as corporate foreplay.

♂ If being a good leader is an aphrodisiac, then I am overqualified.

Lead, Follow, or Quit

An easy way to illuminate your leadership ability is quoting other great leaders. Here is a fun fact you may not have known. Like most famous quotes, the expression, "Lead, follow, or get out of the way" is not directly attributed to any specific leader. It is more frequently associated with Thomas Paine or General Patton. Knowing facts about quotes, now that is something worth bragging about!

♂ Other leaders refer to my opinions as a vision board.

♂ I am not only a leader, but I am also a role model to the mentor of the other leaders.

♂ Employees don't refer to my leadership as effective, but as addictive.

♂ I am not bilingual, but I speak the language of dominance.

♂ I sleep under the stars because ceilings are for weak leaders.

♂ I blinked and started a new trend on accident.

♂ I was born to lead and you were born to follow.

A.R.'s Top 5 Leaders of All Time:

1 **King Leonidas of Sparta** - Mainly because of the movie.

2 **Alexander the Great** - Truly a Maverick of his day.

3 **George Washington** - Because of America... duh!

4 **Winston Churchill** - Bulldog of WW2 and cigars.

5 **D.J.T.** - Greatest President in U.S. History!

Disclaimer: Rankings subject to change based on new movie releases!

♂ People call my leadership style "lightning" because I always take charge.

♂ I don't build leaders, I sculpt legends.

♂ I don't drive results; results spring to catch up with me.

♂ I autographed the company's financial strategy as "daddy!"

♂ I hosted a company seminar and created an epidemic of motivation.

A.R.'s Paraprosdokian

"If feedback is a gift, then it's alright to ask for a receipt!"

♂ I refer to my mistakes as teachable moments for others to learn.

♂ When I join a project, my peers refer to it as a system upgrade.

Word Police!

Here is an easy tip to exaggerate your wisdom as a leader and correct your peers in a respectful way. There is a lot of confusion about the difference between the terms initialism, acronym, and acrostic. This is how you know the difference.

- ✓ **Initialism:** The abbreviation does not form a new word and is referenced as its initials. Example: CIA, FBI, A.R.W.

- ✓ **Acronym:** The abbreviation forms a new word. Example: RADAR stands for Radio Detection and Ranging.

- ✓ **Acrostic:** Is not an abbreviation at all. When a word is referenced as a poetic expression, example: IOWA is referenced as "Idiots Out Wandering Around", it could also be considered a backronym, but that is way too technical.

♂ Regarding my leadership ability, I can, in fact, see the forest through the trees.

♂ I don't take breaks as a leader; I simply allow others a chance to catch up.

♂ My title doesn't make me a leader; I make my title mean something.

♂ I have "skill" tattooed on one arm and "will" on the other because I have the skill and the will to succeed as a leader.

CHAPTER SIXTEEN

ALLERGIC TO SICKNESS

There is a difference between a man claiming he never gets sick and him declaring that, biologically, he is incapable of sickness. Exaggerating our immune system as an atomic bomb ready to destroy germs is normal for men. Tell a man that there is sickness going around the office and you will get a loud scoff followed by a grunt. "I will get sick when pigs fly..." is the common response. When reality catches up, we are the biggest babies on the planet, clutching a tissue box, and begging for meds to relieve our body aches.

When someone accuses you of always being sick, don't settle for a feverish, germ-ridden answer. Always remember, **men don't just exist, they exaggerate**. Respond like this instead...

♂ Doctors told me that my blood type is "W" for "Warrior."

♂ I blow a kiss and high five germs to assert my dominance.

♂ Germs put on gloves when they get too close to my immune system.

♂ My immune system could power a whole city.

♂ I gave a cold frostbite last year.

Shakespeare Style

Try these statements at work. Your boss will let you go home, and you will get to talk with HR.

✓ Thy cruel cough cometh as I am beset by fevers in my loins.

✓ Bid thee farewell workplace, thy shall not attendeth this day.

✓ Deliverables, thou canst demand. Thy plague hath skewered me.

♂ I sneeze antibodies and fart clouds of immunity.

♂ I am allergic to sickness and weakness, lest I repeat myself.

♂ My go-to cure for a sore throat is gargling gravel.

♂ For Christmas last year I gave the flu the flu.

♂ Hospitals use my sweat to disinfect their patient's wounds.

Maximum Nonsense

When in doubt, use vague medical lingo...

✓ I can't come into work today because of my systemic post-viral gastro irregularity.

✓ I would love to attend your party, but I have acute endocrine homeostatic reflux.

✓ Second date, I wish! I can't make it because I am experiencing respiratory somatic depletion with hormonal fatigue.

♂ I once had a virus, and I killed it with my internal dialogue.

♂ I nicknamed my runny-nose a "Victory Drip!"

♂ The common cold tried to sue me for defamation.

♂ My immune system is competing in a strongman competition this fall.

♂ I drink expired milk and eat moldy toast for breakfast, to keep my immune system sharp.

The Prophetic Meteorologist

Because the weather made me do it!

✓ Thunderstorm Bloating: A rare condition where storms make you retain water.

✓ Fog Headaches: When driving to work, the fog interacts with your brainwaves causing a migraine.

✓ Barometric Tendonitis: Changes in pressure make it where you cannot type or move your mouse at work.

♂ I gave chicken pox an identity crisis when I was only eight years old.

♂ I sneeze on petri-dishes to kill all the bacteria.

♂ Doctors make an appointment to see me when they are feeling ill.

♂ An ounce of my blood can cure the plague.

♂ I have trained my white blood cells to form battle formations and conduct air strikes.

Dr. Weston Told You What?

Because you can't argue with a doctor...

✓ He told me to lie naked on the bathroom floor, apply petroleum jelly to my feet, and place a wet tortilla on my head.

✓ He ordered that I hold an ice cube on my left nipple, flap my arms like a bird, and then wrap myself in a silk bedsheet.

✓ I left his nurse's office with directions to boil orange juice, chew on a rotten potato, and say "I'm not sick" three times.

CHAPTER SEVENTEEN

I am an AWARD-WINNING WINNER!

Winning an award for a man is an experience like no other. Plaques, trophies, or ribbons, it doesn't matter what it is, because it is all a reflection of our greatness. Most men have a section of their house specifically designed to display their accomplishments. In our minds, every award is proof of our worthiness to be called a man. Our "Perfect Attendance" award from the fifth grade might as well be the Medal of Honor. The baseball we hit a home run with during the big game in high school absolutely deserves its own custom glass case. Awards don't make the man, but they do glorify the manliness of the man.

When someone asks you if you deserve an award, don't settle for some flimsy modest answer. Always remember, **men don't just exist, they exaggerate**. Respond like this instead...

♂ Last year I bought my trophy case, a trophy case.

♂ I have won more awards for simply being me than you could for pretending to be someone else.

♂ I paid for a carpenter to install another wall in my house for all the awards I have won.

♂ I won Employee of the Year at a company and I don't even work there.

♂ In high school, I was voted the most likely to be the most likely… at winning, everything!

Trophy Wife or Giant Trophy

Choose the giant trophy! Unlike a trophy wife, a huge trophy will never berate you for wanting to play golf on the weekends or roll its eyes when football dominates the television. A trophy wife may sparkle, but a giant trophy illuminates your greatness. An enormous trophy is a proclamation of winning at life, but the tradeoff is that you will likely die alone!

♂ Whoever said, "you can't win them all" has never seen my trophy room.

♂ My participation ribbons have won more awards than you will win in a lifetime.

♂ Award shows have asked if they can use my name to rename their awards.

♂ I have won two Lifetime Achievement awards in a category I wasn't even nominated in.

♂ My trophy room has a table of contents to help my fans know what they are seeing.

Sir Ransom-A-Lot

Knights were known for their armor, swords, and jousting. All the brutality of their clashing on muddy fields frequently came down to a single word, "Glory!" In return for their bravery, knights were rewarded with chalices, jewels, goblets, and best of all, their opponent's armor and weapons. Did you know that knights commonly took their opponents captive and ransomed them for money? Talk about a different type of trophy!

♂ I have been called the Best Man at a wedding I didn't even attend.

♂ I think the only way to use a participation ribbon is to wipe my butt.

♂ I started selling my awards as scrap metal and my trophy room is still cluttered.

♂ The league stopped giving me trophies and started naming the trophy with my name.

♂ My trophy shelf looks like a gladiator's locker room.

Participation Trophies: A Symbol of Mediocrity

We went from fighting in the colosseum, dueling outside the taverns, and clobbering each other in the boxing ring, all the way to shiny plastic tokens declaring that "Everyone's a Winner!" Always refuse to accept a participation trophy. Men don't get awards for existing, they get them for winning! Winners win and losers lose!

♂ I keep all my participation trophies in the permanent filing cabinet, also known as the trashcan.

♂ If I don't stop winning plaques, there won't be any trees left in the rainforest.

♂ I was named "Man of the Twenty-Second Century."

♂ I receive fan mail for my trophy collection.

♂ My chiropractor told me to refuse any more medals due to the neck strain.

How Men View Their Trophies

DON'T BRAG — BRAG A LITTLE — BRAG A LOT — EVERYONE'S A LOSER

♂ I hired another security guard for my trophy room. Three should be enough to guard all that treasure.

♂ I could keep my house warm all winter by only using my awards as firewood.

♂ The Golf Club keeps my jacket measurements on file.

♂ When I travel to award conferences, I bring an extra empty suitcase with me.

♂ If I melted down all my trophies, I could easily create a life-sized replica of the Statue of Liberty.

What Medals Mean

Gold	You are the best!
Silver	You are the first loser!
Bronze	You have a great personality!

♂ The award ceremony to honor me started at dawn and ended at dusk.

♂ My trophy room whispers, "Daddy's home" when I enter the room.

♂ If my accolades were a tachometer, I would be constantly redlining.

♂ I have multiple insurance policies for my trophy room.

Fun Fact With A Bang!

The most prestigious award possible is the Nobel Peace Prize. Ironically, the award is named after Alfred Nobel, the Swedish chemist responsible for the creation of dynamite. If you win this award, your career and legacy will *explode* with excellence.

♂ I don't have a trophy room, I have a trophy warehouse.

♂ There is not enough polish in North America to polish all my trophies.

♂ My employee-of-the-month picture won an award for best picture of an employee of the month.

♂ My award ceremony lasts longer than a traditional Catholic Mass, in Latin.

♂ My last award was not a trophy or a plaque; the constellation Orion was renamed after me.

Goliath's Sword

When David returned to camp after defeating Goliath, what did he do with the giant's sword? That's right! He kept it in the tabernacle. I wonder if David ever offered guided tours of the temple saying, "Oh, and that sword over there is a little trophy of me beating that giant that was mocking God!" Talk about the ultimate manly brag.

♂ I had to rezone my house because my trophy cabinet was too big for the property.

♂ I have more rocks on my championship ring than a quarry.

♂ My handshake won an award for best handshake.

♂ My trophy mantel is made from trophies.

♂ I have won an award for "best typo" in a research paper.

♂ Award show hosts ask me to autograph the podium.

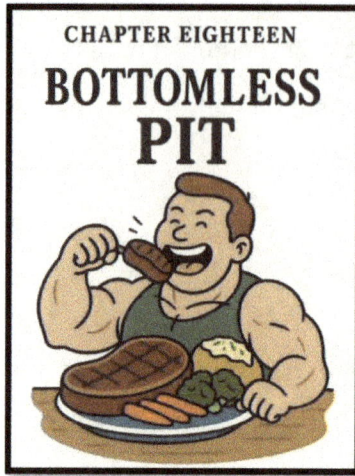

CHAPTER EIGHTEEN

BOTTOMLESS PIT

It is a time-honored tradition for men to brag about their appetites. Our eyes are never bigger than our stomachs. Gigantic steaks, all you can eat buffets, mounds of loaded potatoes...we love them all! It's not about the quantity of food, it's about the willpower it takes to dominate the obstacle in front of us. Watching a man defy anatomy and stretch his stomach beyond human comprehension leaves us with a sense of pride.

While it may be tongue-in-cheek to boldly proclaim, "I could eat the whole cow", it is our manly duty to exaggerate our eating standards. When someone asks about your eating ability don't settle for some lightweight meek answer. Always remember, **men don't just exist, they exaggerate.** Respond like this instead...

♂ I never eat leftovers because there have never been any leftovers at my house to eat.

♂ The only way to calculate my weight after Thanksgiving is using a semi-truck scale at the highway weigh station.

♂ If total calories consumed were a sporting event, I would qualify for Nationals.

♂ I don't eat to live, I live to eat!

The "Real" Food Pyramid

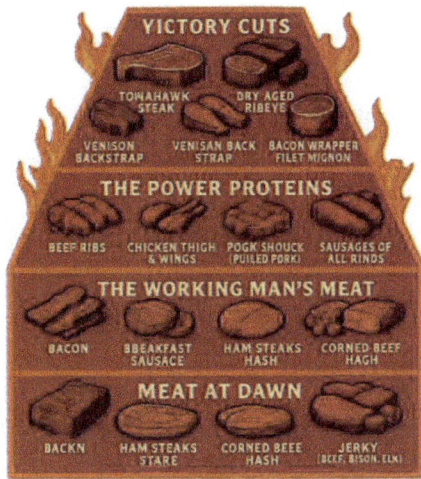

♂   My gravestone will read, "He ate it all!"

♂   I have a custom-made ergonomic fork designed for binge eating.

♂   I am so hungry I could put a restaurant out of business.

♂   I am so hungry I could eat a mammoth without chewing.

♂   I am so hungry I could demolish a steak the size of Texas.

♂   Chefs refer to me as the pantry whisperer!

Brain Horsepower

Did you know that the brain only accounts for 2% of your body weight, but it consumes 20% of your caloric intake? Generating more horsepower means extra food is essential.

Passing Thought: If anyone ever calls you fat, remind them that it's not gluttony, you are simply nourishing a supercomputer located on top of your head.

♂ The city requires me to pay property taxes on my stomach.

♂ Basketball teams retire jerseys to honor players and buffets retire plates to honor me.

♂ I once mistook a family sized lasagna for an appetizer.

♂ My stomach has more square footage than most people's first apartment.

♂ Restaurants regret offering "all you can eat" when I am in town.

Pan-Caked

The Bureau of Advanced Lumberjack Lifestyles and Statistics (BALLS) found that fewer than 3% of adult men could finish ten regular sized pancakes in a single serving. The data shows that percentages drop dramatically as the pancake quantity increases. Do you have the appetite to defy the odds? What do you think about BALLS research?

♂ I refer to the cafe as the gym, my fork and spoon as my weights, and the menu as my workout plan.

♂ When I turned 13, I ate the food pyramid, and it has never been seen again.

♂ Next week I am throwing a potluck... by myself.

♂ I refer to appetizers as the trailer for the main event.

♂ The words "portion control" are not in my vocabulary.

Neverending Bulk Cycle

The concept behind a bulk cycle is to put on a lot of muscle by eating gratuitous amounts of calories. Sure, you gain a little fat, but that's part of the journey. A brilliant heavyweight exaggeration tip is the **Permanent Bulk Cycle**. When you are asked why you eat so much, respond by saying you are on a bulk cycle.

Food for Thought: Think about it... You get to eat as much as you want. People assume you are a bodybuilder and you never have to work out. It's the fitness plan for true champions and you can stay on the couch the whole time.

♂ I refer to calories as casualties of war.

♂ I look at the way black holes eat galaxies as motivation.

♂ When someone offers me "snack size", I start throwing punches.

♂ When I buy in bulk, the grocery store is forced to close until another delivery truck arrives.

♂ My oven turns on automatically when I open the freezer.

Wash it Down

Have you ever noticed in competitive eating competitions, contestants have a cup of water that they dip their food in before taking a bite? This strategy is called "soaking" or "dunking." One way to exaggerate your eating ability is to adopt this professional eating technique during a casual lunch or dinner with friends. Order an extra glass of water and then dip your entrée repeatedly to help it slide down your gullet.

♂ I treat cookbooks like a to-do list.

♂ I never graze, but I harvest all the time.

♂ I clean the plate before I eat the plate.

♂ My diet plan is based on ancient military battle strategy.

♂ The government declared my visit to the buffet to be a natural disaster.

♂ Plumbers refuse to come to my house after taco night.

♂ I leave a restaurant and the table is investigated as a crime scene.

A.R.'s Philosophy on Eating

Food was meant to be for recreation, not for nourishment. Always trust your eyes, they will never be bigger than your stomach. Only grocery shop when you are hungry. Life tastes better when you mix refined carbs and sweets.

Life Quote: "Eat like your ancestors… if your ancestors were competitive eaters or professional body builders."

♂ The buffet manager sent me a cease-and-desist letter.

♂ I order every dish in family size, and then I eat the family.

♂ The plates in my house filed for witness protection.

♂ Your mom refers to me as the human garbage disposal.

♂ Turkeys and pigs send me hate mail every Thanksgiving and Christmas.

The 3 Unspoken Buffet Rules

When you see "All You Can Eat" on a buffet advertisement, have you ever desired to put that to the test? Me too! There are, unfortunately, unspoken rules that most establishments enforce and here is how to avoid being politely asked to leave.

1. Avoid stacking plates ridiculously high like you are in an eating competition.

2. Do not waste large quantities of food. If it's on your plate, eat it.

3. It's a meal, not a marathon. Do not camp at a table for more than 90 minutes.

   **There are no jokes associated with these rules. Please take buffets seriously.

> I asked in my will that my family include a doggy bag in my casket.

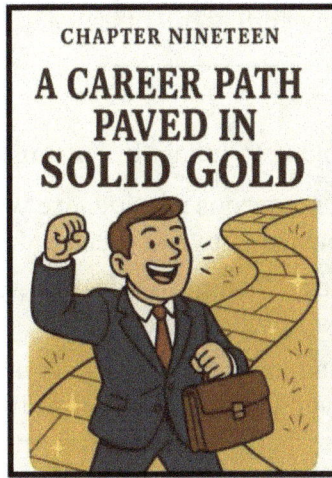

CHAPTER NINETEEN

A CAREER PATH PAVED IN SOLID GOLD

Men have a unique gift of explaining their ordinary career as an epic journey of professional development. An unpaid summer internship at a start-up company morphs into a far-fetched tale of them practically running the business. Sure, the closest we got to the C-Suite was when the boss needed his laundry delivered, but hey, it counts. Handing the CEO his coffee in the morning is a "strategic mentorship with an executive." That's what we say around the dinner table with our family.

It's not lying to exaggerate, it's simply the art of how we tell the story and crafting our own narrative. When someone asks about your magnificent career, don't settle for some entry-level meek answer. Always remember, **men don't just exist, they exaggerate**. Respond like this instead...

⚇ I didn't have to climb the corporate ladder, I took the elevator.

⚇ My job title is so long it requires an intermission to read.

⚇ My business cards have their own currency exchange rate.

⚇ My company's messaging system has my job title listed as "legend."

♂ My social media endorsements have endorsements.

Destination Ego

Three tips for the man looking to inflate his ego in the office:

1. Give yourself a preposterous job title. Are you the Assistant Manager or the Senior Global Executive Associate Manager?
2. Write and rehearse a 20-minute elevator speech. Deliver daily to peers, colleagues, and subordinates.
3. Large print, polished business cards are a must. Hand them out before meetings even if you already know the entire audience.

♂ Peers consider my comments at the water cooler to be keynote speeches.

♂ I broke the glass ceiling and then mounted a spotlight shining back down on my career.

♂ My birthday has been declared a company holiday.

♂ My email signature has more credentials than the royal family.

♂ Employees refer to my meetings as a pilgrimage.

Training Wheels

Here is career advice that will change your life… Send an email to the top three senior leaders in your company offering to mentor them. In the comments, write that you are "happy to help them remove their training wheels." It is extremely important that you provide a due date on their response. The C-Suite loves employees with initiative and this advice is guaranteed to get a response.

♂ Upon a rumor of hiring me, a company's stock price goes up.

♂ My corner office touches all four corners of the C-suite floor.

♂ My resumé is thicker than a phone book and stronger than AR-500 steel.

♂ Co-workers refer to my strategy meetings as prophetic messages.

♂ AI hired me to help it better understand how to explain career success.

Judgement Day

We all fear it, even the best employees. When you sit uncomfortably in a meeting with your boss listening to their assessment of how you did for the year. Receiving a "Year-End Evaluation" can be intimidating. Here are a few tips to help get you through...

- When the review starts, stand at attention and recite the company slogan, motto, and mission statement.
- Bring a framed photo of you and your boss together. Place it on the table for them to see. Refer to the boss as your best friend that would never hurt you.
- **Insurance Policy:** Share with your boss that you may be receiving a serious call at any moment. Stare at your phone the whole time. If things start to go south, grab your phone and storm out.

♂ It is common practice for senior leaders to conclude my year-end evaluation with a standing ovation.

♂ Recruiters from competitors have me on their board of fantasy candidates.

♂ I have a vanity corporate email address for fan mail from the Board of Directors.

♂ I don't brainstorm career moves, I forecast them.

♂ My career trajectory resembles a space shuttle launch.

♂ I don't apply for jobs, recruiters stalk me.

Preach, Preacher!

Let's get serious for a moment. When it comes to a man's career, it is all about vision and execution. He needs a vision, to see the exit door, and execution refers to him getting fired for doing something incredibly stupid.

♂ HR accused me of giving the company whiplash with my career growth and motion sickness with my promotions.

♂ I don't attend meetings, I headline them.

♂ I am so important that if I take a day of PTO, the company goes into a recession.

♂ When I leave a company, they retire the building I worked in to honor me.

♂ I didn't build a career brand, I founded a cult following.

Polishing Your Shrine... I Mean Brand

A good professional brand is what separates the cans from the can-nots. Here are a few tips to help you develop an exceptional personal brand. Use these at work frequently and watch the magic happen.

- ○ **Create a catchy tag line...** "I bring the heat, baby!"
- ○ **Use buzzwords, people love them...** "Synergy, Paradigm, Optimize."
- ○ **Start a work podcast...** because all men these days have a podcast!

♂ The government approved me to mint my own money because they couldn't keep up with my promotions.

♂ The company felt CEO was not a high enough title and declared me their King.

♂ Recruiters ask if they can live stream them offering me a position at their company.

♂ I refer to my project proposals as manifestos.

♂ Companies refer to my promotions as coronations.

Professional Name Dropper

It's not about what you know, it's about who you know. Try these name-dropping strategies and get the respect you deserve.

- ❖ **Accidental Slip:** "Oh, I was hanging out with Bob yesterday, I mean our CEO, Mr. Smith. Sorry he wants me to call him by his first name."
- ❖ **Quotable:** "This reminds me of something Alan, our boss, once said..."
- ❖ **Email Power Play:** "I am copying in our VP, SVP, and EVP to this email chain, for awareness, of course."

♂ My out-of-office messages win writing awards.

♂ The stapler I used in my first job was sold at auction for a million dollars

♂ My side hustles quickly turn into empires.

♂ I refer to my clients as worshippers.

♂ Theatre directors have requested to use my career as the plot for their musicals.

Butt Kissing 101

Here are five surefire ways to kiss butt like a professional:

i. Compliments and flattery will take you far.
ii. Always laugh at the boss's jokes, even if they are not funny.
iii. Adopt the phrase, "That's perfect, I am so glad you are my leader."
iv. "Accidentally" forward an email to the boss where you are praising them. Repeat weekly.
v. Quote your boss in meetings citing them as a "prophet."

People refer to their dream job as a chance to work for me.

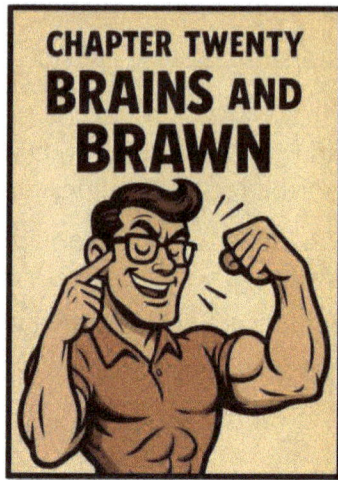

CHAPTER TWENTY

BRAINS AND BRAWN

A wise man knows the perfect opportunity to sneak in a comment highlighting their brilliance when the moment is right. You explain to the less fortunate minds that you didn't become a lawyer or doctor because you were too busy almost getting into a school for rocket scientists. A man doesn't want to be smart or be referred to as intelligent because anything short of being called a genius is an insult.

When someone asks you about your braininess, don't settle for some insubstantial imprudent rebuttal. Always remember, **men don't just exist, they exaggerate**. Respond like this instead...

♂ I am too smart for my own brain to comprehend how smart I am.

♂ I was named a child prodigy because I came out of the womb.

♂ The academic community was shocked when I was the first man to correct a calculator.

♂ I am so smart that I can, in fact, judge a book by its cover.

♂ My genius allows me to make an organic omelet without cracking any eggs.

PHD: Pretty Huge Deal

These days success is not about what you know or who you know, it's about how many abbreviations a guy can put in his signature box. According to the Weston Institute of Exaggeration, there are approximately 27.3 billion credentials in existence. When in doubt, add meaningless letters, numbers, and quotes to the end of your name to earn respect.

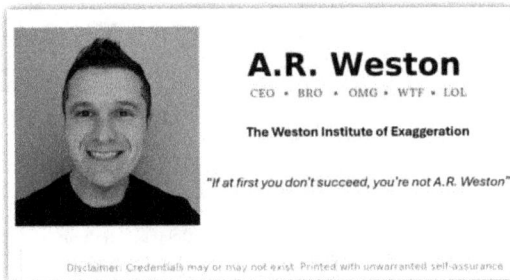

A.R. Weston

CEO • BRO • OMG • WTF • LOL

The Weston Institute of Exaggeration

"If at first you don't succeed, you're not A.R. Weston"

Disclaimer: Credentials may or may not exist. Printed with unwarranted self-assurance.

♂ I can teach an old dog new tricks.

♂ I authored a book called, "How to Un-ring a Bell."

♂ If I wanted to, I could keep a good man down.

♂ I taught myself how to slam a revolving door.

♂ I once stared into a mirror and my genius broke the reflection.

Trivia Night Dilemma

Close your eyes and think for a moment. It's Thursday night trivia at the local bar and the grand prize is free appetizers for a year. The advertisement says you can pick any partner you want. Desperately, you pick up your phone and start scouring contacts. Who do you pick and why?

♂ I once solved an unsolvable puzzle with half of my brain tied behind my back.

♂ I flexed my brain and my jeans ripped.

♂ I am the first man to need four digits to calculate my IQ score.

♂ I am fluent in Spanish, Italian, Latin, and Genius.

A.R.'s Guide to Men's Feelings

Level	Game Type	How Men Feel When We Lose?
Easy	Luck, Matching, Counting, Patterns, Pathways	It's only a game! Then we spend the next few days feeling defeated.
Medium	Words, Letters, Puzzles, Numbers, Logic	We pretend everything is okay. The shame of our father's disappointment plays repeatedly in our heads.
Hard	Strategy, Deduction, Linguistics	Deep self-hatred. Internal crisis. We didn't want to play anyway!

♂ I am the first person to be granted a patent for my thoughts.

♂ When I do crossword puzzles, I don't even need to read the prompts.

♂ My sophomore year in high school, I made the top colleges send me application letters and letters of recommendation. I rejected them all.

♂ I was hired by scientists to fact-check and correct Einstein's notes.

♂ I write subtitles for my thoughts to help others keep up with me.

Skipping Grades?

A pro tip to exaggerating your brilliance is sharing with others that you "nearly" skipped a grade. No one gets hurt and it's beyond fact checking.

110

Here is how it works. When you were younger, "they" said that you should skip fourth grade, but in secret you told the principal you didn't want all the other kids to feel less smart... You are noble and a genius. Works every time!

♂   In my free time I am writing a memoir and publishing it as an encyclopedia.

♂   My voicemail message is a riddle that only I can understand.

♂   I don't resolve problems, I pre-solve them.

♂   The power produced by my brain is measured in horsepower.

♂   I have been banned from trivia night because my brain is considered a lethal weapon.

A Brain Under Construction

Did you know that the male prefrontal cortex does not fully develop until our mid-twenties? We are not immature, we're simply installing wisdom and greatness takes time!

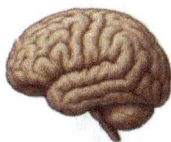

INSTALLING WISDOM

PLEASE WAIT

♂   I don't think outside the box, I engineer and build a new box.

♂   Next year I am planning to write my own algorithm to replace the internet.

♂   My shower thoughts win awards for academic achievement.

♂   I never study history, history studies me.

♂   I taught myself a new language while I was on vacation, over the weekend, at the beach while I was fishing.

Can't Sleep? Me Neither!

There is a clear connection between restlessness at night and brilliance. Likewise, there are countless examples of both modern and historical geniuses struggling to get their ZZZ's. Our brains are wired to constantly think. We feel a compulsive need for control and our dopamine response to stress keeps us in "get stuff done" mode. If you can't sleep at night because of racing thoughts, remember, you are in good company. Some of the smartest people to ever live experienced the same!

♂   My IQ is so high you need a telescope to see it.

♂   I publish a weekly newsletter containing only my inner dialogue.

♂   Friends put on sunglasses when I share my bright ideas.

♂   My professors take notes when I start to speak in class.

♂   I was hired to beta-test spelling and grammar software to ensure it was accurate.

Spelling Bees

Here are seven <u>musts</u> when competing in a spelling bee to appear as the smartest person in the competition.

1. Ask for the definition of the word.
2. Ask for the word's language of origin.
3. Ask for the word to be used in a sentence.
4. Ask for alternate pronunciations of the word.
5. Say the word out loud 10 times before attempting to spell.
6. Spell the word correctly.
7. If you spell it incorrectly, get a liberal arts degree.

♂   I refer to passing tests as granting them mercy.

♂ Last semester I transcribed all my professor's lectures into Latin.

♂ I challenged a calculator to a memory math competition and won.

♂ One of my hobbies is solving paradoxes.

♂ People refer to my memory as a living library because it is so organized.

♂ Critical thinking is for beginners; my thinking is critically acclaimed.

A Paradox Fox

Did you know that there are ten core types of paradoxes? A paradox is something that seems illogical, impossible, or contradicting, but after thinking about it deeply, it may make sense. Studying paradoxes is fun and turns the average person into a philosopher. If you want to impress others by sounding like a logician, yes, a real thing, then I recommend explaining the bootstrap paradox or Einstein's twin paradox to your friends.

♂ Strategists refer to asking me for help as the nuclear option.

♂ My inner dialogue is so powerful it causes tinnitus in people a mile away.

♂ The power of my brain registers on the Richter scale.

♂ People from the future have traveled through time to ask me my opinion.

♂ Scholars have told me that speaking to me destroys their confidence.

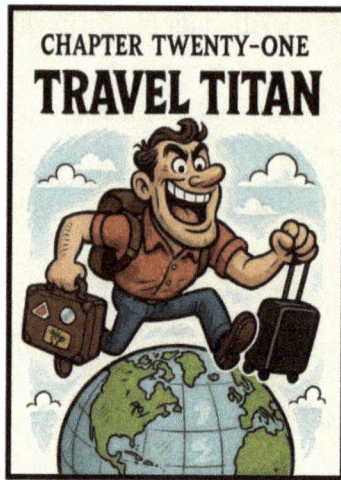

CHAPTER TWENTY-ONE
TRAVEL TITAN

Any man well versed in exaggeration knows that a long layover at an airport in Budapest can be retold as a weekend tour of backpacking in Europe. Likewise, a guy from Iowa does a weekend getaway to Cancun and now obviously knows everything there is to know about Mexican culture. Telling a farfetched travel tale that is bigger than life is not about ego, it is about the thrill of storytelling.

Men know that it's not the length of the trip that matters, it's how you use the time. When someone asks you about your travel adventures, don't settle for some frail modest answer. Always remember, **men don't just exist, they exaggerate**. Respond like this instead...

♂ I visited more time zones in a single week than you have in your life.

♂ I have stamped more passports than a customs agent.

♂ I have been around Europe more times than the plague.

♂ Airports have charging stations reserved for me and bathrooms with my name above the stall.

♂ I backpacked through Amsterdam with nothing on but a smile.

Jet Lag Scale of Truth

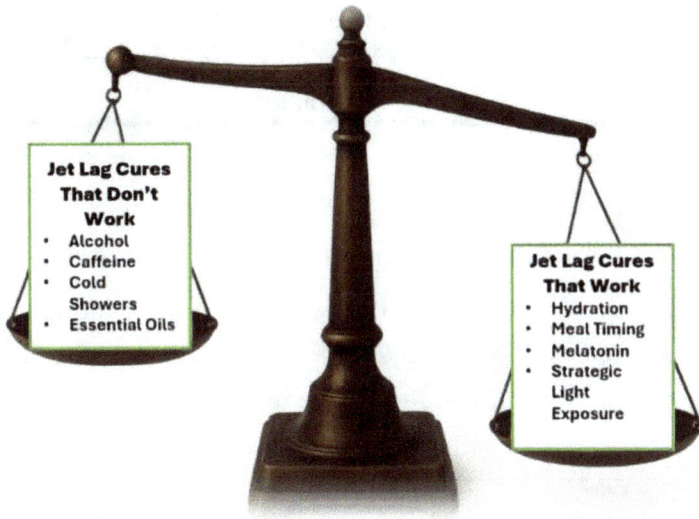

♂ Rum and regret, the two pillars of my travel philosophy.

♂ My passport is so heavy I had to put it on a diet.

♂ The odometer on my tennis shoes just passed 200k miles.

♂ Last year my passport was issued a passport.

♂ I have pick-up lines in eight languages and have been slapped in nine.

♂ I have crossed so many borders that my left nut was granted diplomatic immunity.

♂ I have been pantsed, pickpocketed, and punched all on the same block in Thailand.

The Longest Flights Possible

Come on, I know you are curious...

Rank	From	To	Distance in Miles
1	New York, United States	Singapore, Singapore	9,537
2	Newark, United States	Singapore, Singapore	9,535
3	Doha, Qatar	Auckland, New Zealand	9,032
4	Perth, Australia	London, United Kingdom	9,009
5	Melbourne, Australia	Dallas, United States	8,992
	All over 16 hours of travel time		

♂ I've been to all 50 states, twice in a single week.

♂ When I travel, I buy my souvenirs their own souvenirs.

♂ I am the first man to circumnavigate the world on a unicycle.

♂ This year for Christmas, Santa gave me my own time zone in honor of all my traveling.

Free Airport Hack

Traveling is stressful. Waiting in security lines, expensive food, and getting comfortable is challenging in those rigid chairs. Next time you travel, bring a medium-sized bowl in your carry on. Ask one of the fast-food places for a couple of cups of hot water and a few packs of salt. At the gate while you wait, fill the bowl with water, add the salt, and give yourself a warm footbath. Sit back, relax, and I bet you will even get tons of stares as other travelers admire your genius. Men will respect you, women will admire you, and security might even ask you a few questions.

♂ In airports, other travelers will ask me for directions to the baggage claim because they know I am a travel legend.

♂ My living room furniture is an airplane seat for a recliner and an airport lounge bench for a couch. It's the only way I feel at home.

♂ I ask customs agents what is in their bag because I know their country's laws better than they do.

♂ The layover on my last trip lasted longer than your marriage.

Clean Hiney – DIY Bidet

Did you know that French luxury is only a quick trip to the hardware store away? All you need is a dual hose connector, two feet of garden hose with an on/off valve, and a single zip-tie. Your budget and your backside will sparkle like the Eiffel Tower on Christmas!

♂ My passport is thicker than an encyclopedia and has more stamps than an elementary school Valentine's Day party.

♂ The airport terminal charges me monthly rent because I practically live there.

♂ My luggage has seen greater things than you have seen in your dreams.

Pack Like a Man!

These tips are guaranteed to get a "thank you" from your wife...

✓ **Time Management:** Always wait until the last minute before you start packing.
✓ **Financially Savvy:** Pick the smallest bag possible and suggest you share to save money on baggage fees.
✓ **Organized:** Pack 3 of the same outfits in different colors.
✓ **Creative:** Bring only mismatched socks and roll them into your shoes.
✓ **Thoughtful:** Remove "some" of her packed clothes the night before the trip and tell her on the way to the airport that you optimized her wardrobe.

I have skinny-dipped in every lake in Minnesota.

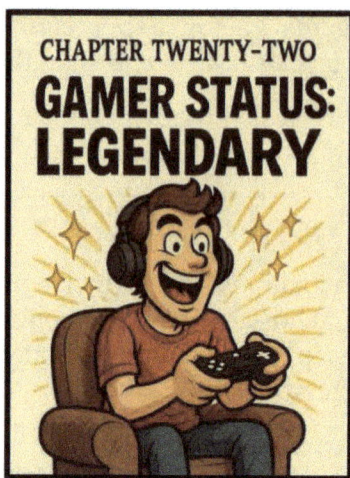

CHAPTER TWENTY-TWO

GAMER STATUS: LEGENDARY

Turn down the lights, turn the volume up, grab your remote, and follow me to the ultimate manly proving ground. A gaming console is not a toy, it is a rite of passage for men. Reflexes... Check. Strategy... Check. Trash talking... Check. If you know, then you know that you know. The swagger of a true gamer is undeniable and raw. A famous poet once said, "When gaming, the minutes turn into hours, and the hours into days, and who needs to shower anyways."

Mom told us as kids that we were throwing our lives away sitting in front of the TV, but she lied. We found a new life filled with adventure, action, and fun. When someone asks you if you're any good at "gaming", don't settle for some hopeless noob answer. Always remember, **men don't just exist, they exaggerate.** Respond like this instead...

♂ I have never played a game that I didn't dominate.

♂ The fan club of my kill streak grows every day.

♂ I refer to every player as a noob, even if they have been playing for years.

♂ I refer to my controller as "My Magic Wand!"

♂ The last time I saw "Game Over" on the screen was... I have never seen this blasphemy.

Play With Yourself

There are several benefits to playing video games solo. For starters, learning to play in a low-pressure situation will help you build comfort in your game. Please spend time building the skills and strategic thinking required to play the game before you add real life competition. Playing with yourself is both enjoyable and will prove as an advantage in time.

♂ There are scholars rewriting history books right now to capture and document my gaming legacy.

♂ It is a ritual that when I lose a game, my remote gets thrown at the screen until it breaks. I've had the same screen for 10 years now.

♂ Game manufacturers create secret advanced levels for me because the normal game is always too easy.

♂ A video game company reached out asking if they could use my avatar as the final boss in their new game.

Noob-Bashing

All men have experienced it and all men have done it. When playing a new game the first couple of times, we encounter trash talk from our friends or even more likely, from complete strangers online. Noob-bashing is part of the gamer experience. Don't lose heart; soon you will learn the game and then a fresh batch of noobs will start playing that you too can insult.

♂ My mouse filed assault charges against me because my reflexes are too fast.

♂ My opponents uninstall the game when I respawn.

♂ I broke the space time continuum with my click per second rate.

♂ My PC doesn't buffer, the universe simply lags to keep up
with me.

♂ Levels beg me to unlock them and I graciously do.

Hands Off My Joystick

There is nothing closer to a gamer than his joystick. A man's joystick is a
symbol of power, precision, and overcompensation. It is taboo in gaming
culture for another man to touch another man's joystick without permission.
Remind all your gaming buddies that they can look, but they can't touch.

♂ I have never needed a patch; the games patch themselves
when I start playing.

♂ I don't level up, I evolve.

♂ Textbooks have been written about my gaming ability.

♂ Every win is considered a flawless victory.

♂ The final boss asks for a rematch after I beat him.

How Many Consoles?

Did you know that there are approximately 333 different gaming consoles
and platforms created since 1948? That means on average there are 4
platforms created on an annual basis.

Other gamers bow down before me... but I don't let
them kiss my feet because they are not worthy.

CHAPTER TWENTY-THREE

THE TECH LORD

What was dubbed nerd culture 20 years ago is now one of the coolest things you can say about another man. We are not tech-savvy, we are Tech Lords bringing to the masses salvation by troubleshooting even the most complex system issues. Coding, writing script, debugging, or simply telling a lost soul to restart their computer... we can do it all. When it comes to technology, the age of AI does not scare us because no system will ever beat us.

Let's be honest, do we know it all? Probably not. It's not about knowing it all, it's about the willingness to learn and dominate something new when it comes to technology. When someone questions you about your technological intellect, don't settle for a glitched, crashed answer. Always remember, **men don't just exist, they exaggerate**. Respond like this instead...

♂ I refer to coding as combat and my keyboard is my weapon.

♂ I don't have to refer to my desk as a workstation, it is a brag-station.

♂ Every time I code, an AI angel gets its wings.

♂ I refer to myself as a tech cowboy and coding is my six shooter.

♂ During a first date, I explain algorithms, API integration, and software updates.

Tech Lord Nerd Tidbit

During the mechanical era of the 1840's, Charles Babbage created the "Analytical Engine" and his partner, Ada Lovelace, wrote the first algorithm.

♂ Automation is not my skill, it is my personality.

♂ My father drilled for oil and I drill for data.

♂ I didn't choose coding, coding chose me.

♂ I am such a techy that my laptop is considered a weapon of mass computation.

♂ I don't code, I write sweet poetry with my keyboard.

Geek Factoid

Did you know that the first computer bug was a literal bug? Back in 1947, a moth crawled inside of a concept computer and the engineers logged their notes as a "bug" being found.

♂ I named my sons Python and Prada.

♂ My love language is "technology."

♂ My system is not the only thing that runs distributed systems, so does my ego.

♂ I am such a techy even my one liners are overengineered.

♂ I am such a techy that my dating profile is read-only.

Byte-Sized Nugget

Worldwide, the general public produces more than 300 million terabytes of data! Considering the first hard-drive built in 1956 had a maximum capacity of 5 megabytes puts things into perspective.

- ♂ People refer to my attitude as parallel processing.
- ♂ I am not trying to brag, but I can format a C drive in less than five minutes.
- ♂ I never gossip, I push consistent updates to the public.
- ♂ I could debug an entire system before you could write a single line of HTML.
- ♂ I am the guy you call when IT support cannot help you!

CHAPTER TWENTY-FOUR

HUNTING CHAMPION

Spending the morning in a duck blind or deer stand is exactly what a man desires for his Saturday. It's cold outside and the sun has started popping up from beyond the horizon. There is a thermos filled with coffee and a rifle sitting in our lap. Life does not get much better than hunting. A ten-point buck approaches at 200 yards and we prepare our shot. BAM! BAM! The sound of bullets fling through the air as the deer nonchalantly looks around and then casually trots away. We only missed because we intentionally pulled our shots high and to the left, or at least, that is what we will say later to our buddies.

Our stories will never be about failure...no way! We are expert sharpshooters and woodsmen. Our hunting tales must be filled with manly bravado. When someone questions you about your hunting ability, don't settle for an inaccurate, underpowered answer. Always remember, **men don't just exist, they exaggerate**. Respond like this instead...

♂ On my last hunting trip, the deer shot itself so it could take a selfie with me.

♂ Lions and bears have asked me to author a book on how to hunt to learn my techniques.

♂ My hunting calls are so good that they summon conventions of animals to my blind.

♂ If an animal looks in the mirror and says, "ghost" three times, then I will show up with my rifle.

♂ I would like to bring back mammoths so I can taxidermy one for my wall.

♂ I could hit a moving target from a helicopter using a two dollar pistol.

Pickled, Stuffed, and Mounted

The art of taxidermy is seriously misunderstood. Trophy animals are not stuffed like a teddy bear. Their skin is carefully removed, dried, and treated in preservatives. Once the skins have gone through the pickling process, they are mounted on polyurethane foam molds. The taxidermist will then adjust the foam until the animal looks as life-like as possible. Taxidermists are the real artists and deserve a fine arts award!

♂ The only scope I need is my right eye and two pieces of steel.

♂ I write love poems on all my arrows and aim for the deer's heart.

♂ Animals send me invitations for their family reunions and I get invited back every year.

♂ I have been told that turkey, deer, and rabbits have a fan club, and I am their favorite hunter. They are dying to meet me.

♂ My wife refers to me as the "meat man" and it's not what you think, I am also good at hunting deer!

♂ A tree once cut off its own branch, sharpened it, and handed it to me as a gift calling me, "The Lord of the Hunt."

♂   I never shoot a warning shot at bears; I show them my trigger finger and they run away.

Know Your Ranges

Deer Hunting Rifle	Hunting Range (Yards)	Maximum Range (Yards)
.30-06 Springfield	300 – 600	3,500
.308 Winchester	300 – 500	3,500
.270 Winchester	300 – 400	3,500
.243 Winchester	200 – 300	3,000
.30-30 Winchester	100 – 200	2,500

♂   My hunting dog started a charity for the family of the ducks I hunted last year.

♂   Rabbits wake up in the middle of the night having nightmares that I am hiding in their burrow.

♂   My footsteps are so silent that I have literally snuck up on ghosts in the woods.

♂   I have bagged a buck so big that it wouldn't fit in the back of a semi-truck.

That Stinks, Bro!

Did you know that scent travels differently at dawn compared to dusk? In the morning scents carry downward and opposite in the evening due to thermal currents. If you need to exaggerate your hunting knowledge, start with thermodynamics and olfaction science.

♂   My favorite animal to hunt with my crossbow is a mosquito and I never miss at 100 yards.

♂ I have a unique hunting technique called bare-handed bear hunting. It's like it sounds and I always take home my prize.

♂ The game-warden once gave me a ticket so he could get my autograph.

♂ My hunting license doesn't have my name on it, it says "LEGEND" and has no expiration date.

Did You Hear That?

Elk, deer, and other game animals detect ultrasonic frequencies that humans cannot hear. Something as simple as a jacket zipping or a rifle being adjusted and you may as well be playing a tambourine. Here are a few easy tips to up your hunting game:

➢ Use electrical tape on any contact points.

➢ Choose brushed cotton or fleece jackets.

➢ Slow and steady movements.

♂ I once shot a buck at 400 yards and the does gave me a standing ovation.

♂ I can shoot the wings off a fly at 100 yards with a BB gun.

♂ I never use scopes because they are for people who can't feel the wind or sense the elevation.

♂ I hunt deer using ricochet shots only. Straight shots are too easy.

♂ One of my hunting dogs is named Buck Norris and the other's name is Major Magnum.

Elevation, Windage, and Luck

Hunting with a rifle or bow is all about controlling what you can control and accepting what you cannot control. As expert hunters, we adjust elevation to overcome the vertical and tweak windage to account for the horizontal.

What we cannot predict is small gusts of wind, errors in calculating drop, and if the projectile flies true.

The Hunter's Serenity Prayer

God, grant me the serenity
to accept the shots I don't make,
the nerve to hold back my tears,
the courage to take the shots I might hit,
and the wisdom to exaggerate the wind when I miss.

♂ I can outshoot a sniper with a borrowed rifle in the dark.

♂ Government scientists are currently studying my grouping pattern to understand the full potential of men.

♂ I can zero a rifle that I am not even shooting.

♂ I was kicked off the range because the instructors said I was intimidating them with my shooting skills.

Scope Kissed

A scope kiss occurs when a hunter's face is positioned too close to the scope, the rifle recoils backwards, and the eye is struck. Typically, this results in a nasty shiner that lasts a few days. A scope kiss is also the sign of a novice shooter. If a scope kiss ever happens to you, then try explaining it like this...

- "I was testing the durability of my scope with my face."
- "I am training for my next fight."
- "My rifle loves to give me a little action... literally!"

CHAPTER TWENTY-FIVE
THE KING OF MANLY HUMILITY

A wise leader once said, "If another man thinks he is better than me, then I have no place for his arrogance on my team, I will destroy him with my humbleness." Men have developed a special talent for bragging about being the most humble man on the planet. It is common to hear a man boast about the time he scolded a man for not demonstrating meekness. Broadcasting humility as a badge of honor is something that only the ultra-egotistical have mastered. Spotting a humble-bragger is not difficult as they may be seen stooping down graciously, and with touching restraint, let us know how humble they are compared to the ordinary person.

If anyone ever alleges that you are as humble as a peacock in a parade, don't settle for a flimsy modest answer. Always remember, **men don't just exist, they exaggerate**. Respond like this instead...

♂ I am so humble that I was nominated to be King of Manliness and I declined, twice.

♂ I once destroyed another man with my humility.

♂ Mirrors apologize to me because they cannot reflect my true greatness.

♂ At my funeral, I requested that no one be allowed to talk about my greatness, only how humble I was.

♂ I am so incredible that my ego can be in two places at the same time.

Confident or Arrogant Douchebag?

Two men are chopping firewood for the winter. One man remained quiet and lets the pile tell the story of his hard work. The second man yelled, "Hey, look at how big my pile is; I am a hard worker!" The first man earned respect, and the second man demanded it. Confident men walk upright while arrogant men puff out their chest! The lesson is... don't be an arrogant douchebag!

♂ I pray for the Pope, that he will one day be as humble as me.

♂ When I look in the mirror, I avoid eye contact with myself to avoid overwhelming myself with my significance.

♂ I whisper compliments to strangers to make them feel better about being around someone as handsome as me.

♂ The Romans asked if they could build a statue of me to replace Caesar and I turned them down, twice.

♂ The Catholic Church asked if they could canonize me as a saint, but I turned it down because it would be unfair to the other saints to be compared with me.

Make Them Know You're Humble...

If arrogance is the focus on self, then the only true way to be humble is to serve others. A great way to demonstrate humility is to focus on other people's needs. That way, other people can see how humble you are and they will give you the praise you deserve. Friends will worship you. What a great roadmap to humility!

Author Note: Please disregard the guidance above. Drinking and writing books do not mix. The recommendation of serving others to gain worship from friends is vain and conceited. These views probably do not reflect the views or opinions of the author.

- ♂ The dictionary redefined the word "silence" to describe what happens when I walk into a room.

- ♂ When I am on stage, spotlights are turned off because they are dim compared to me.

- ♂ Congress asked me if I would autograph the original Declaration of Independence to make it worth more.

- ♂ The monks built a shrine to my humility, but I don't let anyone visit it because they are not as good as me.

- ♂ I installed a filter on my phone that edits out people that don't look as good as me. All I have on my phone is selfies now.

The Humility Index

$$H = G + M / D$$

$$\text{Humility} = \frac{\text{Gratitude} + \text{Meekness}}{\text{Declarations of humility}}$$

- ♂ When I sing, angels take notes, but I ask them to never repeat the words because they would never sound as good.

- ♂ I am so humble I give regular people credit for all the great things I have done.

- ♂ I declined being awarded the title "Man of the Millenia" because I felt the title was demeaning.

- ♂ My humility has ended wars and cured diseases. I needed you to know that.

- ♂ I let others take credit for inventing sliced bread because I am so humble.

Loquerisne Latīne?

Did you know that the word humble comes from the Latin word humilis? The original meaning described being low to the ground. Over time, the word began to describe lowliness in relation to noble society. Brag about your humility while explaining Latin lexicology and philology.

♂ I ghostwrite books about humility to keep people from knowing how great of a writer I am.

♂ I once turned down a handshake from the Pope because he was not worthy of touching my hand. He agreed!

♂ My resume is written on a napkin and says "trust me." I never get turned down for a job offer.

♂ Scientists have tried to clone me but said they could never duplicate my level of humility.

♂ I received a standing ovation for a speech I gave about humility and I sat down to show the crowd I was more humble than them.

Doing it Ghandi Style

Without a doubt, there are few examples of living a humble life that come remotely close to Ghandi. He lived a simple life built on serving others, sacrifice, and forgiveness. If you need a way to exaggerate humility, then nothing will get the attention of others like saying, "I could teach Ghandi a lesson on humility." You may also get a slap and an eye roll!

♂ I am so humble that I turned down playing the role of Zeus in a blockbuster movie because it was not a big enough role.

♂ I correct my friends when they call me humble because it understates my level of humility.

♂ When I won the award for "Most Humble," I turned it down because "HUMBLE" was not written in all caps.

♂ I am so humble and amazing that I can whisper to the wind and it will blush.

♂ I refused to be knighted because the King was not worthy to touch my shoulder with his sword.

Phishing For Compliments

This section is not how it sounds. This section is about how you prompt others to give you undeserved compliments. Okay, so it's exactly how it sounds. Here are a few go-to methods to receive tons of compliments.

> - **Ask Innocent Questions**: Do you think I look too good today?
> - **Make Unnecessary Apologies**: I'm sorry my looks make you feel less attractive.
> - **Downplay Impressive Things**: I know I always win the gold medal, but anyone could do it.
> - **Only Request Feedback When Things Go Well**: When I threw the winning touchdown, how well did I throw the ball?

♂ My parents erased my face from family pictures because it made them all look hideous.

♂ I am so humble I let others blow out the candles on my birthday cake to make them feel important, too.

♂ I am so humble that I apologize to doorways for walking through them because my marvel breaks the hinges.

Five Proven Ways to be Humble

I. Commission a statue of yourself and donate it to a local charity.
II. Publicly share compliments that your boss gave you with coworkers.
III. Write a memoir titled, "I'm The Man You Wish You Were!"
IV. Offer to teach a class at work called, "How to be worthy, like me!"
V. If you are a leader at work, declare your birthday a company holiday, and you are the only one that gets the day off. Make your employees use their vacation time off.

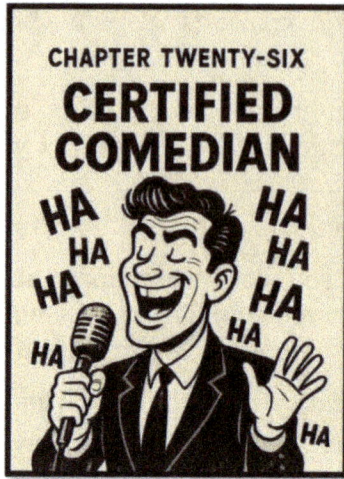

CHAPTER TWENTY-SIX

CERTIFIED COMEDIAN

Since Adam told the first poop joke to Eve, men have been inspired to say ridiculous one-liners to get laughs. Everyone knows there is nothing better than a side stitch from laughing too hard. Men don't tell jokes, they reshape reality with a solid punchline. The ability to use humor to lighten moods, uplift others, and capture people's attention is one more tool in the arsenal of a man. Guys know when they are funny! Ironically, guys that are not funny don't always know that they are indeed unfunny, and that is funny!

If you received a nickel every time a guy declared "I should do standup", you would at least have $2.25 by now. Bottom line, we all think we are hilarious with perfect joke delivery! If anyone ever compares your sense of humor to stale bread, don't settle for an awkward lackluster response. Always remember, **men don't just exist, they exaggerate**. Respond like this instead...

♂ I have told jokes that didn't land, they ascended.

♂ I have cracked a joke so hard that the earth quaked.

♂ A barista told me, "I'm not looking for a serious relationship," so I told a joke. Now we have a baby registry.

♂ I am such a natural comedian that even my awkward silences have punchlines.

♂ If laughter is the best medicine, then consider me a pharmacist.

The Perfect Dad Joke

Writing the perfect dad joke requires four things. First, a tacky pun. Second, paralyzing predictability. Third, genuine innocence. Fourth, it must guarantee an eye roll from the listener. If anyone tells you to stop making dad jokes, never quit pun-ching back.

♂ I am so funny that I make peoples' reflections laugh.

♂ I can tell a joke to someone sleeping and they will giggle in their dreams.

♂ I told the joke to the self-checkout and it gave me all my groceries for free.

♂ I am so funny that I made the barista at the coffee shop shoot milk out of their nose and I hadn't even ordered yet.

Colosseum of Comedy

What man doesn't love the Roman Empire? Apparently, the Toga Roadies liked a good joke. Two guys named Hierocles and Philagrius created the first joke book in the 4th century. Add this to the list of why we all cherish the Tunic Titans.

♂ I am so funny I have made people laugh in elevators that I wasn't even in.

♂ My sense of humor is so dark that I rub it in lotion and it lives in my basement.

♂ I once told a pigeon a clean joke and it turned into an eagle. I told the eagle a dirty joke and it turned into a buzzard.

♂ I can make a toddler stop crying with a single joke because that is my level of maturity.

♂ My sense of humor is so dark that I created a will that says "figure it out" and a treasure map that leads to a bomb range.

Gallows Humor

Sometimes an innocent joke goes wrong. You know the moment when the punch line drops and someone softly says, "That's dark, bro!" As the joke-teller, do you apologize and retreat? Do you double down and tell another joke? Who knows, maybe your friends will *die* laughing after they hear the second joke!

♂ My sense of humor is so dark that I surprised my grandmother in the nursing home with a gravestone that had a pre-inscribed date of death.

♂ I am so funny that I started charging my psychiatrist and parole officer to hear my jokes.

♂ My sense of humor is so dark that when I joke about "burying the past", it's not a metaphor.

♂ My idea of a good practical joke involves pulling the fire alarm during a wedding and chaining the doors shut.

Mostly Harmless

A good practical joke should bruise a man's ego, but never his body. The goal is to get a laugh, not commit a crime. Here are a few mostly harmless practical jokes to try out. Pack your buddy's shower head with green powdered food coloring and create a sewer shower. Put a "For Sale" sign on your friend's new car with the price of **FREE – Just Ask!** Be careful though, what goes around comes around!

♂ I am so funny that the Ouija board didn't tell me my future, but it did tell me a joke.

♂ My sense of humor is so dark that my guardian angel left me with a 1-star review, so I sent him to hell.

♂ I am so funny that I tried to be serious, and the universe whispered "LOL, pass" into my ear.

♂ My sense of humor is so dark that I always start a first date with a joke and it ends with a shovel.

♂ My sense of humor is so dark that my idea of a good practical joke is getting my parents audited by the IRS for tax evasion.

Malapropism

The idea behind a malapropism joke is the use of an incorrect word intentionally inserted into the wrong sentence. For example, "That guy is a wolf in cheap clothing", or "My buddy is a suppository of information." It takes cleverness and sophistication to pull off a proper malapropism. Only those that graduate Magna Carta can do it!

♂ My sense of humor would make the Grim Reaper blush.

♂ I am so funny that my eulogies turn into roasts and even the widow applauds.

♂ I am so funny that I treat interviews like open mic night.

♂ I am so funny that if you listen to me tell jokes for four hours, you may need to go to the emergency room to treat an erect sense of humor.

♂ I am so funny that my puns have ended wars and my one-liners have started them.

♂ My sense of humor is so dark that when someone says "there is a light at the end of the tunnel", I show them a picture of someone being hit by a train.

♂ I told the divorce judge a few dad jokes and received full custody, alimony, the house, and the dog. Let's just say he wasn't too judgmental.

The Sense of Humor of a Cactus

A dry sense of humor is like coarse sandpaper. When it's in the right hands, it gets the job done, but application is everything. If you do have a dehydrated wit, that's okay! Please remember not to fling metaphorical sawdust in everyone's eyes when you tell a joke.

♂ I am so funny that I had to give the audience cue cards to stop laughing.

♂ I am so funny that my awkward silences deliver the best punchlines.

♂ People call me the laugh pharmacist and I have been over-prescribing medicine with no limit on refills.

♂ My dad jokes come with a lifetime warranty.

Premature Punchlines

We have all been there! The mood is right, the buildup is going smooth, and the timing is near perfect. We are about to release a joke loaded with charisma and shock value. Then it happens, a premature punchline comes shooting out at the wrong time. Embarrassed and weeping in the corner, we are told it's okay. It could happen to anyone, but it's a shameful moment for a man. This section has no point, but to help those that suffer know that they are not alone!

I grew up as the class clown and now I am the Dean of Dad Jokes!

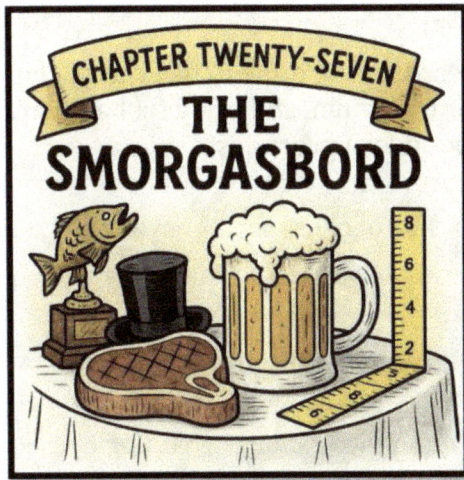

CHAPTER TWENTY-SEVEN
THE SMORGASBORD

No matter what is going on in life, there is always a naysayer, doubter, or skeptic nearby. There is always an opportunity for a man to exaggerate his circumstances. Whenever you are asked about your abilities in anything else in life, exaggeration is the key to the best responses. Check out this list of extra exaggeration one-liners.

Always remember, **men don't just exist, they exaggerate!** Here is a smorgasbord full of ways to respond instead...

♂ My pee has been known to purify entire river systems into fresh drinking water.

♂ I only wear cologne that's fused with gunpowder and the tears of my critics.

♂ The weather man calls me to ask permission before issuing a thunderstorm warning.

♂ Golf Club managers build their greens based on the blueprints for my lawn.

♂ I entertain my yard nightly with a choreographed light show, music, and sprinkler system.

♂ I use kerosene as aftershave and gasoline as mouthwash.

Grocery Bags

Did you know a standard plastic grocery bag can hold up to 17 pounds? If you load bags to their maximum, and carry six bags per hand, then you are carrying about 200 pounds of groceries!

♂ When rain touches me, it converts into steam.

♂ I am considering buying a continent this year as a birthday gift to myself.

♂ I paid to have a time-zone changed because I was tired of getting jet lag.

♂ I chase my chaser with a chaser that was chased by another chaser.

♂ People ask if alcohol has built a tolerance to me.

♂ The drinks I pour are so smooth that jazz music immediately starts when I pull out a bottle.

♂ I bought a single brick to use as a stress ball.

A.R.'s Shower Thoughts

- A fitted sheet is only possible to fold once a person has consciously accepted that a fitted sheet is impossible to fold.
- If you hit something with a hammer when it is broken and it does not magically fix itself, then did you not hit it hard enough?
- If a pimple is unreachable on your back, does the pimple still deserve to be popped or should it be left to taunt you?

♂ Whoever said, "you can't buy love" didn't have as much money as me.

♂ If you can't take wealth with you, then why is my hearse towing a bank vault?

♂ I bought a swamp and converted it into a world-class golf course for the tax write-off.

♂ Landscape designers use my yard as a case study for feng shui.

♂ I regularly lick the floors and handrails in substations to test my immunity.

♂ I can outrun a cold on foot.

♂ I declined a request to make my lawn a world heritage site because the title was not prestigious enough.

Holy Cow

Did you know that an average cow weighs around 1,200 pounds and roughly 500 pounds of that is meat? The rest of the cow is used for animal feed, glue, pharmaceuticals, and the hide is used for leather products. Nothing goes to waste!

♂ I have a person on staff whose job it is to open my wine bottles.

♂ Publishers ask me to save my emails to write a biography of the best businessman ever born.

♂ When I take a bathroom break, global stock prices plummet.

♂ The local buffet nicknamed me the "Demolition Dude."

♂ Halfway through medical appointments, the doctor sits on the table and asks if I can give them a check-up.

♂ If you boil my sweat and breathe in the vapors, then your body will be 100% detoxified.

♂ Dental floss, a toothpick, and a paperclip. That's all I need for fishing tackle.

♂ My puns are so sharp, my family must wear safety glasses around the house.

♂ My jokes are so dry that my nickname is "the drought."

♂ I once caught a hawk, taught it to speak, and then released it back into the wild.

♂ I once trained a shark to eat vegan.

Throat of Thunder

The longest recorded burp lasted over a minute. A normal belch is less than 5 seconds in length. Anything over 10 seconds is exceptional!

♂ My go-to alarm clock is a bear trap.

♂ The social security office let me pick my own number.

♂ Security companies pay me to protect their headquarters.

♂ I chewed through a box of nails that was seasoned with charcoal powder.

♂ The power of my sneeze is stronger than a hurricane.

♂ I curled a tree trunk, and the forest begged me to stop.

♂ When my clothes are wrinkled, I flex and the wrinkles disappear.

♂ I fought the Old Faithful geyser with shop towels and won.

♂ I tame avalanches with a firm voice.

♂ I squatted with a moose on my back to win a bet with myself.

♂ I once knocked the malarkey out of another man.

♂ Habanero juice is what I use for eye drops.

♂ The leaky faucet in my bathroom drips the highest quality whiskey.

Dripping Sweat or Manly Cologne

There are approximately 3 million sweat glands on a man's body and for highly active guys this creates about a gallon of sweat per day. Sweat is about 99% water mixed with a little sodium, urea and other trace minerals. Most colognes are 90% water mixed with alcohol. A man sweating shouts, "I'm relatable." A man wearing cologne expresses, "I care about you." A man should desire to do both!

♂ I entered a staring contest with the eye of a hurricane, and it blinked first.

♂ Cologne companies mix in drops of my sweat to make their products an aphrodisiac.

♂ The FAA fined me for creating sonic booms with my farts.

♂ The best therapy is gunfire and explosions.

♂ Commercial airlines use my spit as rocket fuel.

♂ My chef had to file for workers' compensation after a week of me ordering appetizers.

♂ I can shoot a bullet out of the air with another bullet.

Duct Tape To the Rescue

Here are five random things you can use duct tape for that most people don't know.

- ➤ **Waterproof patches:** Fix small leaks in a poncho, air mattress, tent, or pool float.
- ➤ **Blister Protection:** Mold a small piece to the back of your ankle or toes to prevent friction.
- ➤ **Lint Roller:** Wrap your hand sticky side up and pat sweaters, jeans, or fleece jackets.
- ➤ **Fire Starter:** Roll into the shape of a candle wick. Burns hot and slow.
- ➤ **Emergency Bandage:** Great for temporarily splinting broken bones and stopping bleeding.

♂ I can shoot through the hole of a donut while it is falling from an airplane.

♂ I can always get what I want, when I want, however I want, and I do it with humility and grace.

♂ I consider myself a Type A+ personality.

♂ I once went to the deepest cave on earth to make others feel more elevated.

♂ I won a staring contest with myself because I cannot keep my eyes off myself.

♂ In caves, the guide is only allowed to whisper my name because saying it at normal volume will cause an echo.

Jet Fuel, You Make My Motor Sing... But Not in a Good Way

Fun fact that every man needs to know. You wouldn't benefit from using jet fuel in a gasoline powered car, although it's fun to say and the concept sounds awesome. Jet fuel is kerosene based and closer chemically to diesel. Long story short, it would destroy your injectors! If you want to exaggerate what you run in your car, say, "race fuel with an octane over 110."

♂ Researchers study my footsteps to prove that legends do exist.

♂ I can set a broken bone using duct tape and rebar.

♂ I once carved a Red Oak into a Number 2 pencil using a dull knife.

♂ I gave frostbite a sunburn.

♂ I fall asleep to rock music and my alarm is heavy metal.

♂ I never have to clear my calendar because my calendar clears itself out of respect for my schedule.

♂ My last barber needed a spotter when he combed my beard.

♂ I could stop a charging rhino with a fierce gaze.

♂ Last year I left a mark on a scar.

♂ I tip valet drivers with stock options and real estate investment opportunities.

♂ I once paid for a luxury yacht with stock options.

♂ I may skip dessert, weddings, and foreplay, but I never skip leg day.

♂ Even the worms in my soil attended the finest colleges and wears designer suits.

♂ The three pillars of my leadership are caffeine, confidence, and flattery.

A.R.'s Field Guide to Scents

TOP THREE	BOTTOM THREE
1. PIPE TOBACCO	1. LAVENDER
2. LEATHER	2. JASMINE
3. CEDARWOOD	3. ROSE

♂ I could drain the dragon on a nation's flag and their GDP would go up.

♂ Ghosts in my house are known to call a priest to help them get rid of me.

♂ Water taken directly from glaciers is not as pure and fresh as me.

♂ I have more testosterone than a man riding a three-armed grizzly bear.

♂ I refer to midnight snacks as famine relief.

♂ I could eat the whole herd right now.

♂ Multi-vitamin companies grind up my toenail clippings to help increase their product's potency.

Barefoot – The Way God Intended It

Every man is searching for the perfect pair of shoes, but all you must do is look to what God gave you already. The potential benefits to barefoot training is improved posture, a stronger lower body, and less impact on your joints. Give it a try and see what you think!

♂ I have been exposed to more germs than a preschooler walking barefoot through a daycare.

♂ My white blood cells filed a lifelong restraining order against germs.

♂ I can clean a fish using nothing but my sharpened toenail clippings.

♂ When I toast at a wedding, the glasses at other weddings clink themselves in my honor.

♂ I drink with so much prestige that orchestra instructors stand to clap.

♂ I refer to my first plate at the buffet as the prequel and the final plate as the sequel. I am the main character.

♂ I taught the rock how to roll.

♂ I have multiple anvils on my desk at work, I use them as paperweights.

Is Riding a Grizzly Bear "Actually" Possible?

Of course it is! This is a book about exaggeration, but there is a catch and no one has ever tried twice. Anatomically, bears have the skeletal structure and strength to carry a man on their backs. Hypothetically, a man could ride a bear through a sunny meadow singing kumbaya and playing a ukulele. Now the catch, a bear would object to being ridden forcefully. Hopefully, whoever is taking the pictures is quick and there is EMS close by. Seriously though, don't try this. It will not go well for you! Now hold my beer while I ride this grizzly!

♂ I can turn pocket lint into a loaf of baked bread.

♂ The sun challenged me to a staring contest and we are still playing.

♂ My car door only squeaks because it's begging me to lube it up.

♂ My last barber used a machete to find my chin.

♂ The shelves I installed during an earthquake are more level than the ones in your living room.

♂ My punches are known to lower sperm count and my kicks reascend nether-berries.

♂ I kicked a soccer ball, and it evolved into a real ball, a football. If I kicked you, maybe you would evolve into a real fighter!

♂ With rain water and a few peppers, I can make a world-class hot sauce.

♂ My favorite flavor of beef jerky is ambition lightly salted with humility.

♂ I can make bricks by stomping gravel into sand.

♂ All my tools are engraved with my name, social security number, religion, and blood type.

Is Your Pepper Natty?

The hottest naturally grown pepper, the Ghost Pepper, long held the title of World's Hottest Pepper. The pepper game changed after 2007 as engineers designed new hybrid super-peppers that pushed the Scoville units into unchartered territory. This begs the question: is your hot pepper sauce natty?

♂ I am the first man to light a cigar using a volcano.

♂ I can shave my beard with a chainsaw while riding a unicycle.

♂ I once stared at the man in the moon until he blinked.

♂ I traded in my snowblower for a flamethrower.

♂ I am so rich that before I flirt, they must sign an NDA.

♂ My 401k hits harder than your daddy issues.

♂ I could whistle into a cave and cause an avalanche on the mountain above.

♂ I enjoy kicking a hornet's nest because I like the way the stings tickle my feet.

- ♂ My pocket knife is the size of a machete, and my machete is the size of a samurai sword.
- ♂ My beard is so thick it has more volume than a gospel choir.
- ♂ I never let anyone borrow my tools without a liability waiver and an ironclad contract to return them.
- ♂ My motorcycle helmet is forged out of AR-500 steel.

Magnet Fishing

Step aside other hobbies, a new, epic time waster has arrived to save men from boredom. Welcome to magnet fishing! All you need is a powerful magnet, strong rope, and the heart of a treasure hunter. Get you some!

- ♂ I reinforce water balloons with rebar before I throw them.
- ♂ I can turn sand into a glass vase by squinting at it too long.
- ♂ I once yelled at a tsunami, and it retreated into the ocean.
- ♂ I can peel an orange with a chainsaw.
- ♂ Give me a volcano and a piece of meat and I will grill you a five-star meal.
- ♂ I could cook a sirloin steak using a manhole cover and a blowtorch.
- ♂ I have my cake and eat it too, all the time.
- ♂ I can sneeze while I squeeze the trigger and still hit center mass every time.
- ♂ When the scope fogs up and my hands are shaking from the cold, I still hit the target with perfection.
- ♂ I don't aim, I use my intuition to bend the laws of physics.
- ♂ I only wear gray clothes to help others be more noticeable around me.
- ♂ My salad spinner is two bear traps welded together.
- ♂ I would swim, while bleeding, across shark infested waters, for a coffee refill.

♂ When I walk in the lumber section of the hardware store, my chest sprouts new hair.

Exotic Pet Flex

There are a handful of places in the United States with zero laws banning exotic pets. That means a guy could theoretically have a lion in his backyard, a crocodile in his pool, and a pet cobra in his bedroom. This is not recommended, but perhaps a way to exaggerate your manliness if you happen to live in a state that allows it.

♂ I pet wolverines and cliff dive to unwind after a busy week.

♂ I disciplined insomnia and put it to sleep.

♂ I don't solve problems, I dismantle them and take their dignity.

♂ Scholars plagiarize my random thoughts and publish them to win academic awards.

♂ I fought a ghost and sent him to the afterlife again.

♂ There is more testosterone in my little finger than a stampede of bulls.

♂ My couch cushions are stuffed with cash and stitched together with gold laced thread.

♂ My muscles are bigger than a combine tractor and harder than an anvil.

♂ I am the first leader to make a meeting agenda blush.

♂ I've never been stumped as a leader; I pause for dramatic effect to let others think they know what they are doing.

♂ The trophies I win are so big they are shipped in multiple boxes and require assembly instructions.

♂ You could iron the whole laundromat on my abs.

♂ My uppercut will make you earn frequent flyer miles.

♂ Wolves declare me as their pack leader when I go camping.

149

♂ It is common for me to pitch a tent in my tent.

Macho Mentions

- o If you can't fix it, then build something better.
- o The person put in charge is the one that remains calm when everything is going wrong.
- o Above all other qualities, the ability to make others laugh is the greatest talent.

♂ I could put out a wildfire by whispering "simmer down."

♂ I can paddle upstream without a paddle.

♂ I once paddled a canoe across the Pacific with nothing but a broken shovel.

♂ My marriage ended because I spent more time checking bags at the airport than I did at my kids' sports games.

♂ My butt has touched more toilets in foreign countries than flight attendants eating ice cream with dairy intolerance.

♂ When I fish in the ocean, Great White Sharks wave white flags and put up signs that say, "You win!"

♂ I throw one cast with an empty hook, catch two fish, and a third voluntarily jumps in my boat.

Born to Lead?

Question: What is the timeline to become a leader?

Answer: There is no timeline, lead from day one.

- ❖ Lead yourself,
- ❖ Lead the team,
- ❖ Lead the business!

Don't wait for permission. Leadership starts with you.

♂ I taught Mother Nature Morris Code and now thunder speaks to me.

♂ I once insulted a bear by nicknaming it "marshmallow" and then when it got upset, I roasted it over a campfire.

♂ I could chop down a forest with a spoon.

♂ I trained a grizzly bear to roll over and play dead.

♂ I could plow a field using a canoe and a pair of chop sticks.

♂ Pinecone is my favorite deodorant scent.

♂ I could sharpen a knife using only my chiseled chin.

♂ I can grow a complete garden by whispering "grow" at the dirt.

♂ I have carved a new canoe out of a large tree by chewing.

A Manly Character – Wisdom For You!

- Learning to listen is the first step in learning to lead others.
- A man that chases power will find it and he will be bitterly disappointed with his catch.
- Always fix your own posture before attempting to fix others' misperceptions.

♂ I once cracked a walnut by pressing my pinky fingers together.

♂ I can find water in the desert and turn it into ice cubes.

♂ When camping is over, I put out the fire with a backhand and spit.

♂ I can put the genie back in the bottle and demand three more wishes.

♂ I dressed a lion in a tutu and taught it to purr.

♂ I could break a steel beam over my leg.

♂ I could hammer a nail into hard wood using only my shin.

♂ I prefer steel wool for a toothbrush. I made a chili so spicy that the crockpot spontaneously combusted.

♂ I once yelled at a grizzly bear and now it is in therapy.

Three Types of Men

Always trust the ancient Greek's wisdom...

The ancient Greek philosopher, Thárros, once said that there are three types of men. "The first man sees a beehive and runs away screaming. The second man runs up to the beehive and kicks it. The first man is a coward, and the second man is an idiot. The third man is wise and records them both on his cellphone, then he uploads to the internet to make a viral meme."

♂ My preferred way of opening coconuts is bashing them against my skull.

♂ I can scare away a rattlesnake by whispering "BOO!"

♂ My boss told me to dress for the job I wanted, so I came to the next meeting without a shirt on.

Thank You For Reading

A special thanks to everyone that made it this far, congratulations. You have been through a journey exploring all the ways that men exaggerate and stretch the truth. My hope for you is that you laughed, rolled your eyes a few times, and maybe even had to look up a few things to check if what you were reading was true. Hey, full transparency, even some of the "facts" were a bit embellished and inflated.

Thank you for laughing and playing along. It's all meant to be good fun. Everything in our lives these days is so divided that laughter should bring us together. I want men to approach their manliness with swagger, poise, gravitas, bravado, pride, and machismo. Likewise, men must also value humility, honor, integrity, and duty to their families. This book was a lot of fun to write and I hope you enjoyed it.

Always remember, *men don't just exist, they exaggerate!*

— A.R. Weston

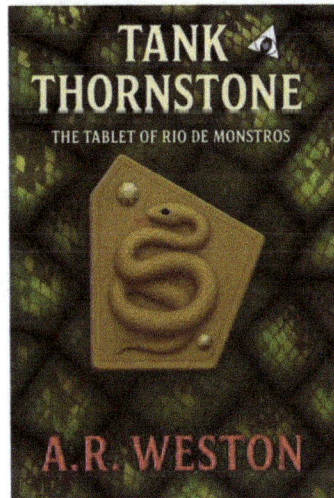

www.ingramcontent.com/pod-product-compliance
Lightning Source LLC
LaVergne TN
LVHW022340080426
835508LV00012BA/1293